DANIELL

MW00627691

DAILY
DOSES

31 Days of Inspiration for Healthcare Professionals

Limits of Liability and Disclaimer of Warranty
The author and publisher shall not be liable for your misuse of this material. This book is strictly for informational purposes. The purpose of this book is to educate and entertain. The author and publisher do not guarantee anyone following these techniques, suggestions, tips, ideas, or strategies will become successful. The author and publisher shall have neither liability nor responsibility to anyone with respect to any loss or damage caused, or alleged to be caused, directly or indirectly by the information contained in this book. Views expressed in this publication do not necessarily reflect the views of the publisher.

Printed in the United States of America

Keen Vision Publishing, LLC
www.keen-vision.com
ISBN: 978-1-948270-45-8

Contents

A Note From The Nurse

Hello, healthcare professionals! I'm Danielle Barnes, a family nurse practitioner currently serving in Huntsville, AL. In addition to being a nurse, I am a Christian. When I began my journey in healthcare, I searched for devotionals to encourage me on my journey. Unfortunately, I realized there weren't many devotionals specifically for healthcare professionals. So, I decided to write one!

Working in the healthcare field is incredibly rewarding, yet extremely challenging – mentally, physically, and emotionally. *Daily Doses* is a 31-day devotional designed to provide encouragement and moments of devotion for people just like you and me. In this devotional, you will find practical, biblical, and insightful tips to make every day at work a great day, despite the obstacles you may face. Each day is equipped with a devotional, a daily dose of quotes or affirmations you can recite throughout the day, and a prayer to jumpstart your daily conversations with God.

As you journey through this devotional, remember that you are not alone in your struggles as a healthcare professional. There are thousands of men and women just like you across the world who deal with many of the trials you face. Allow this devotional to be a resource and daily dose of inspiration as you strive to be the best healthcare professional you can be.

Remember that God is with you. He has graced you for this beautiful life assignment. Your time in His presence, reading this devotional, and praying will rejuvenate you and give you the strength you need to keep going. I pray you enjoy Daily Doses. If you know a healthcare professional, be sure to share this devotional with them as well!

With Love,

Danielle

Starting Your Day

How do you prepare yourself for the day? Do you start by hitting the snooze button a dozen times before getting out of the bed? Do you stress out about the busy day ahead? Do you spend your morning dreading the next several hours you will spend at a job you despise with people you can't stand? Maybe, you are one of the lovely few who leaps out of bed because you are super excited about your job.

The most impactful thing we can do is starting the day off right. How your day ends depends on how you start it. So, how do you start your day off right? First, you must decide to have a great day. Contrary to popular belief, you do not have to be a morning person (or a "night owl" for all of my night-shift friends) to choose to have a great day. Optimism is deciding to look at the glass half full, rather than half empty. It is choosing to believe the best and be positive. Even when the day seems impossible, optimism allows us to look at the challenges we face in a different light. Through the lenses of optimism, problems become smaller, and solutions become crystal clear. Second, you must spend time with God. Whether it is five minutes or five hours, any time with God is time well spent.

Talk to Him about your upcoming day. Tell Him about your worries and concerns and allow Him to give you grace and peace to handle whatever comes your way. Talk to Him while you're eating breakfast, driving to work, or even once you get to work.

I keep a devotional in my work bag, so if I don't get my time with God at home, I can talk to Him and pray before I start seeing patients. Additionally, ask the Holy Spirit to teach, guide, lead, and assist you. Isaiah 11:2 says, "And the Spirit of the Lord will rest on him— the Spirit of wisdom and understanding, the Spirit of counsel and might, the Spirit of knowledge and the fear of the Lord." With God on your side, there is nothing you can't do, understand, or complete. Lastly, encourage and build yourself up by declaring the Word of God over your day.

Philippians 4:13 states, "I have strength for all things in Christ Who empowers me [I am ready for anything and equal to anything through Him Who infuses inner strength into me; I am self-sufficient in Christ's sufficiency]." This scripture reminds me that I am powerful, ready for anything, and strengthened through Christ. When I read this, the nurse in me is drawn to the word *infuse*.

The word *infuse* reminds me of how intravenous (IV) fluids work. IVs are long needles medical professionals use to give patients medication or fluid replacement. When I use IVs, the fluids are directly inserted into the patient's body for quick relief/replenishment. That's exactly what Jesus does for us daily. He infuses the strength we need to endure and handle our day.

Dose for the Day

Make these declarations and choose to have an awesome day!

- God is on my side – therefore, I cannot be defeated.
- Satan wants to load me with cares, but God wants to load me with benefits daily.
- I walk in love, and I am quick to forgive at all times.
- The Lord has filled me with the Spirit of God, and He has given me wisdom, ability, and expertise in all things concerning my job.
- I am more than a conqueror through Christ Jesus.
- I am triumphant in every situation I face because God always causes me to triumph.
- I will be a success because the God of heaven will help me succeed.
- In Jesus, I have perfect peace and confidence. I am of good cheer.
- I have perfect knowledge of every situation because God is with me and will help me.
- I will make the right decisions at the right time.
- I will overflow with confident hope through the power of the Holy Spirit.
- I am graced for every shift/every day that I work.
- I am prepared for this job. I am anointed to handle whatever comes my way.

Daily Prayer

Father God,

Thank You for this beautiful day. This is the day that You have made, and I choose to rejoice and be glad in it. Thank You for a new and fresh start. You have given me everything that pertains to life and godliness. I will have a great day! Direct my steps today, and let no sin rule over me. I pray over every conversation and activity that I will engage in today. Strengthen me in every area where I feel weak and help me when I do not know what to do. Grant me the grace to do my best, no matter the situation. I choose to work with enthusiasm because I work for You, rather than people. Thank You for going ahead of me and preparing the day. I have no reason to be afraid or stressed. You have not given me a spirit of fear, but a spirit of power, love, and a sound mind. I expect great things today. In Jesus' Name, Amen.

Scriptural References: Isaiah 11:2; Philippians 4:13, Psalm 118:24; Exodus 35:30-31; Romans 8:37; 2 Corinthians 2:14; Nehemiah 2:20; John 14:27; Romans 15:13; 2 Peter 1:3; Psalm 119:133; Ephesians 6:7; Ephesians 3:16; Deuteronomy 31:8; 2 Timothy 1:7

Difficult People

Mood killers. Debbie downers. Grouchy guys. Every job has its share of these types of people. They would make your life so much better if they quit their jobs. They are often irritable, demanding, pessimistic, short-tempered, cranky – just overall difficult. It can be easy to identify the coworkers you aren't too fond of, but take a second and do some self-inventory. Are you a difficult person to work with? What is it like to deal with you at work?

I'll use myself as an example. Usually, I am a bubbly, fun, and energetic person. Even during tough situations, I try my best to stay optimistic. However, when I was working as a registered nurse during my last semester of nurse practitioner school, I was overwhelmed and stressed. The smallest inconveniences would frustrate me. I treated my unfair coworkers just as they treated me. I was cold and my attitude was less than pleasant. I would mumble under my breath when something got on my nerves. The worst part was that I did not care. One day, I was so overwhelmed, and I knew I needed to pray. As I prayed, God encouraged me to lean on Him for help with everything – dealing with difficult people, included. You see, it is crucial to invite God into every part of your day. When you face negative patients, unfair supervisors, or disrespectful co-workers, respond with kindness and compassion. Keep in mind that you are not responsible for the actions of others; you are responsible for how you respond.

Over the years, I've learned that everyone is battling with something. Often, those in our work environments are dealing with issues that aren't work-related which can cause them to be grumpy, negative, or snappy. This is why prayer should be your initial response to everything. In the Bible, 1 Timothy 2:2 tells us to pray for those in authority. According to Matthew 5:44, you are to pray for those who want to make things worse for you. Praying will keep your heart clean from grudges and bitterness. If while praying you realize that you need to apologize for being cold or saying something that wasn't nice, do it – don't hesitate! Make things right.

While working as a travel nurse, I encountered another nurse who was very difficult to work with. Some days, she was the charge nurse, and she was rude, condescending, unfair, and brash. No matter how nice or helpful I was to her, she treated me horribly. Every time I worked with her, I would cry the entire drive home. I began to pray for her. I prayed that God would heal the bitter areas in her heart that caused her to mistreat others. Shortly after I began to pray for her, she put in her two weeks' notice. When we do our part, God will certainly do His. Psalm 138:8 says, "The Lord will perfect that which concerns me."

Dose for the Day

Think of a difficult coworker or manager/supervisor. Pray for them and perform an act of kindness today at work.

Daily Prayer

Father God,

Thank You for the job, place, and season I'm in right now. I know that there is no such thing as a trouble-free job, but some days it seems as if dealing with imperfect people is too much to handle. Help me walk in love and be kind, especially when it is not reciprocated. Help me to be wise and use good judgment in my actions, words, and thoughts. I pray for those in authority over me. Your word says that the king's heart is like a stream of water directed by You, and You turn it wherever you please. I thank You for favor with those in authority over me. Give me the grace to interact with them, even when I don't agree with the decisions they make.

I pray for every person I work with. May my coworkers feel Your love and peace. Touch their hearts and heal the bitterness from past hurts they may have experienced. Bless them in every area of their lives. I pray that they will come to know Your love through me. Even though it seems really hard to do, Your word says that with You, nothing is impossible. I choose not to be moved by what others do for Your ways keep me stable. Your word says that You will cut off the strength of the wicked but You will increase the power of the godly. I pray that I do not become weary, anxious, or stressed, but that I will experience Your grace, love, joy, and patience as I interact with my coworkers. Thank You for Your ever-present help and presence in my life. In Jesus' Name, Amen.

Scriptural References: 1 Timothy 2:2; Matthew 5:44; 1 John 2:6; Psalm 138:8; Matthew 10:16; Proverbs 21:1; Psalm 119:161 (Message translation); Psalm 75:10; Matthew 19:26

What's Love Got To Do With It?

Love is one of the most important, yet misunderstood words EVER. What is love? What does it look like? Love is mentioned in the Bible over 500 times. Love is a big deal. Knowing what love is and how it impacts us is vital for Christians. We are instructed to love God with all of our heart, soul, mind, and strength. Loving God helps us care for others, which is vital in our field of work. 1 Corinthians 13 is known as the "love chapter" and simply defines love. It says, "Love is patient and kind. Love is not jealous or boastful or proud or rude. It does not demand its own way. It is not irritable, and it keeps no record of being wronged. It does not rejoice about injustice but rejoices whenever the truth wins out. Love never gives up, never loses faith, is always hopeful, and endures through every circumstance. "

We cannot talk about love without talking about God. God is love. Love is not something that He does – He is love. 1 John 4:9-10 says, "God showed how much he loved us by sending his one and only Son into the world so that we might have eternal life through him. This is real love – not that we loved God, but that he loved us and sent his Son as a sacrifice to take away our sins." Have you ever questioned if you are loved? From now on, every time you question His unconditional love for you, look at the cross. Look at the ultimate sacrifice that was made with you in mind! Jeremiah 31:3 says, "I have loved you with an everlasting love; I have drawn you with unfailing kindness." In addition to all of that, 1 John 3:1 tells us that he loves us so much that he calls us his children!

Since we know that God's nature is love, there is no reason for us to struggle with fear and anxiety. God is not fear. God is not harsh. God is not angry with you. He is love. It is imperative that we catch this revelation and apply it to our everyday lives. Fear and love cannot coexist. According to 1 John 4:18, "Such love has no fear, because perfect love expels all fear. If we are afraid, it is for fear of punishment, and this shows that we have not fully experienced his perfect love." If we are struggling with fear or anxiety, it could be because we are not fully convinced of His love for us.

A couple of years ago, I was in a weird place. I was in the middle of nurse practitioner school, burned out from my job at the time, actively serving at my church every week, and trying to maintain a healthy social life all while becoming increasingly anxious about finishing school on time and life after graduation. I was an emotional mess. One night, I was studying, and I began to cry. I talked to God about how I felt, and His words changed everything. He told me, "Your belief in me is connected to your belief in my love for you and what I will do for you." If we don't believe that He loves us unconditionally like He has told us (and displayed to us), then it is impossible for us to believe or trust Him to do what He has promised. Don't make the mistake of confusing God's love with human love. God is not like man. Isaiah 54:10 says, "'For the mountains may be removed and the hills may shake, but my lovingkindness will not be removed from you, nor will my covenant of peace be shaken,' says the Lord who has compassion on you." God's love is consistent, unfailing, unshakable, unchangeable, and everlasting. His love for us is so grand that we can never fully understand or describe it. Ephesians 3:18-19 describes it like this: "And may you have the power to understand, as all God's people should, how wide, how long, how high, and how deep his love is. May you experience the love of Christ, though it is too great to understand fully. Then you will be made complete with all the fullness of life and power that comes from God."

Receive God's love today. Know that you are loved by God and there is nothing you can do to undo His love for you. Receiving His love helps you to love others. You can't give to others what you do not have. 1 Corinthians 13:13 tells us that faith, hope, and love will endure, but love is the greatest of these. God loves you. Never forget it!

Dose for the Day

Make these declarations about love today!

- I am loved by God, for God is love.
- The love of God is in my heart by the Holy Spirit.
- I walk in love. I am rooted and grounded in love.
- God loves me regardless of how I perform.
- I choose to trust and rest in His love for me.
- I trust God's love to carry me through my day.

Daily Prayer

Father God,

Thank You for Your love. I choose to love You above all things. Your word says that the greatest commandment is to love the Lord my God with all of my heart, all of my soul, all of my mind, and all of my strength. Help me to realize that You love me unconditionally, even when I do not feel loved. I pray that my eyes would be enlightened and I can see Your love for me in every area of my life. Help me to receive Your love, so that I can love others. Your word says that You are love and all who live in love live in God, and God lives in them. Help me to take the love You have given me and give it to others. Your unfailing, unconditional, and consistent love can reach me no matter where I am.

In Jesus' Name, Amen.

Scriptural References: 1 John 4:9-10; Jeremiah 31:3; 1 John 3:1; 1 John 4:18; Isaiah 54:10; Ephesians 3:18-19; 1 Corinthians 13:13; Romans 5:5; 1 John 4:7; Ephesians 3:17; 1 Corinthians 13:4-7

Loved People, Love People

I f we love God the most, we will love others best. Because you are unconditionally and totally loved by God, you are already enabled and equipped to love and show love to every single person you encounter. Like I mentioned in the last devotional, love is mentioned over 500 times in the Bible (depending on the translation). However, "love one another" is mentioned only about 11 times.

Walking in love isn't a suggestion; it is a command. According to John 13:34, Jesus said, "Let me give you a new command: Love one another. In the same way, I loved you, you love one another. This is how everyone will recognize that you are my disciples—when they see the love you have for each other." Mark 12:30-31 says, "And you must love the Lord your God with all your heart, all your soul, all your mind, and all your strength. The second is equally important: 'Love your neighbor as yourself.' No other commandment is greater than these." We can only love others to the degree that we love ourselves. Simply put, if you don't love yourself, you cannot effectively love others. Since we are children of God, we are supposed to love. 1 John 4:7 tells us, "Dear friends, let us continue to love one another, for love comes from God. Anyone who loves is a child of God and knows God." What does loving others look like? Jesus gives us the perfect example. John 1:14 says, "So the Word became human and made his home among us. He was full of unfailing love and faithfulness. And we have seen his glory, the glory of the Father's one and only Son." Jesus came to earth in human form so he could relate to us and establish relationships with us. He died for us, which is the ultimate expression of love.

Jesus hung out with those who were considered no-bodies, outcasts, lames, unpopular, and less than. He dined with sinners and was scolded and judged for it. When asked about it, Jesus gave the perfect response. In Matthew 9:12, He replied, "Healthy people don't need a doctor—sick people do." Jesus was humble, kind, and compassionate. He loved all people, no matter what.

When you and I love others how He loves, we will become an attraction to those who do not know Him. His love is how others recognize us as Christians. Trust me, I know that loving others is not always easy. It can be down-right tricky at times. However, our love walk must line up with what and who we say we believe in. Grace helps us love others like Jesus! We are to love people the way Jesus loves us, not how we want to love them. To perfect your love walk, you must go against how you feel. You cannot love God and not love people. Love is important to God, and it should be important to us.

Colossians 3:12-14 says, "Since God chose you to be the holy people he loves, you must clothe yourselves with tenderhearted mercy, kindness, humility, gentleness, and patience. Make allowance for each other's faults, and forgive anyone who offends you. Remember, the Lord forgave you, so you must forgive others. Above all, clothe yourselves with love, which binds us all together in perfect harmony." Love trumps all. Out of love flows compassion, grace, kindness, forgiveness, contentment, and joy. My father always told me that one way to show love to someone is to pray for them. Praying for others takes your mind off of yourself.

Another way to show love is to display kindness. A compliment or a warm greeting goes a long way. Even when you disagree, respond in love – not with a loud sigh and rolled eyes. 1 Corinthians 13:4-7 pretty much sums everything up:

Love is large and incredibly patient.
Love is gentle and consistently kind to all.
It refuses to be jealous when blessing comes to someone else.
Love does not brag about one's achievements nor inflate its own importance.
Love does not traffic in shame and disrespect, nor selfishly seek its own honor.
Love is not easily irritated or quick to take offense.
Love joyfully celebrates honesty and finds no delight in what is wrong.
Love is a safe place of shelter, for it never stops believing the best for others.
Love never takes failure as defeat, for it never gives up.

Dose for the Day

Make it a point to pray for your coworker(s), even those who have offended you, talked about you, or took advantage of you.

Daily Prayer

Father God,

I pray that the more I receive your love, I will be free to love others. You are love and have enabled me to love. Help me to practice love today with everyone I encounter. Let my actions and words line up with Your loving nature. Help me as I clothe myself with tenderhearted mercy, kindness, humility, gentleness, and patience. I pray that my life will be filled and overflow with the power of Your love that I may bring You honor. Help me to love as You love. Help me not to judge or look down on others. Thank You for equipping me to face every day with Your gracious power. I love You, Lord, and I thank You for loving me. In Jesus' Name, Amen.

Scriptural References:
John 13:34; Mark 12:30-31; 1 John 4:7; Matthew 9:11-12; Colossians 3:12-14; 1 Corinthians 13:4-7

Always Be Kind

We are called to be kind. Being kind is also a choice we each have to make daily. Proverbs 3:3-4 says, "Never let loyalty and kindness leave you! Tie them around your neck as a reminder. Write them deep within your heart. Then you will find favor with both God and people, and you will earn a good reputation." The word *let* implies that we have control over how we act. No one's behavior should control our actions. *Then* implies that after we do as the scripture says, we will find favor and earn a good reputation. Are you experiencing favor with God and other people? If not, ask yourself, "How have I been treating others? What is my attitude like?" Genuine kindness opens the door to favor.

So, what exactly is kindness? Kindness is NOT being cold, rude, snappy, moody, not speaking to others, refusing to smile, unconcerned, selfish, showing no interest or mean. Kindness is the quality of compassion and generosity, characteristic of God's dealings towards the weak and poor, and demanded of believers. Kindness is also shown in the words and deeds of Jesus Christ. Being kind means to be helpful, compassionate, gracious, polite, generous, affectionate, thoughtful, friendly, to smile, and to listen attentively. We are called to be kind even when it inconveniences us, and when it is not the most popular thing to do. Go the extra mile to show kindness and compassion.

Jesus is the perfect example of kindness. He was even scolded for being kind. Matthew 9:10-13 says, "Later when Jesus was eating supper at Matthew's house with his close followers, a lot of disreputable characters came and joined them. When the Pharisees saw him keeping this kind of company, they had a fit, and lit into Jesus' followers. "What kind of example is this from your Teacher, acting cozy with crooks and riffraff?" Jesus, overhearing, shot back, "Who needs a doctor: the healthy or the sick? Go figure out what this Scripture means: 'I'm after mercy, not religion.' I'm here to invite outsiders, not coddle insiders." Jesus dined and hung out with those who were considered "bad." It was not the best group to fellowship with, according to human opinion. Guess what? Jesus did not care. He chose kindness over being popular and upholding religious rituals.

Kindness is a fruit that is produced in us when we allow the Holy Spirit to control our lives. Galatians 5:22-23 says, "But the Holy Spirit produces this kind of fruit in our lives: love, joy, peace, patience, kindness, goodness, faithfulness, gentleness, and self-control. There is no law against these things!" Kindness must be a part of every single day. Colossians 3:12 tells us, "Since God chose you to be the holy people he loves, you must clothe yourselves with tenderhearted mercy, kindness, humility, gentleness, and patience." For some of us, it is challenging to display mercy, kindness, and patience – especially when kindness is not reciprocated. Grace helps us to be nice to those we don't believe deserve a kind gesture. As healthcare professionals, we HAVE to be kind. We must value people, period. We cannot say that we love God, but are mean to people. It doesn't work like that. Here are a few ideas to show kindness at work that I have tried:

- Occasionally, bring a treat for everyone to share and enjoy.
- Communicate your appreciation to your coworkers and supervisors.
- Help an overwhelmed coworker with his or her tasks.
- Give compliments often.
- Smile often.
- Pray for a patient having a difficult time.
- Be a listening ear to an anxious team member.
- Take a coworker who is having a bad day to lunch.

Dose for the Day

Before you begin your day, ask God, "Who can I bless today?" When your day is over, ask yourself, "What did I do today to make someone's day better?"

Daily Prayer

Father,

I thank You and praise You for being kind, patient, and compassionate towards me. Thank You for showing me what real kindness means and what it looks like. Help me to respond in love. Help me to show kindness, mercy, compassion, love, and patience every day and in every situation. Remind me that kindness is not a suggestion, but a command. Help me to be kind to those who are unkind to me. I know that I am not responsible for the actions of others, but I am responsible for my responses and reactions. Romans 12:13 tells me that "when God's people are in need, be ready to help them. Always be eager to practice hospitality. " Help me not to be selfish, but to recognize and always be ready to help those who need it. Give me creative ways to display kindness in the workplace. Give me the strength to show compassion to those I care for, such as my patients and their families. Thank you, Father, that you comfort me so that I may be a source of comfort for others. Help me to be the best example of kindness through my smile, attitude, love, and actions.

In Jesus' Name, Amen.

Scriptural References: Proverbs 3:3-4; Matthew 9:10-13; Galatians 5:22-23; Colossians 3:12; Romans 12:13; 2 Corinthians 1:4

Workplace Tea

Every work environment has at least one Chatty Cathy. You know, the person who somehow knows everything about everybody, is always in someone else's business, is always talking, but rarely does his or her work. All of the rumors in the workplace usually trail back to the same old gossiping person. Gossip, unfortunately, is pretty common in healthcare. Not only do we work with many people, but we also must bear hearing the personal information of patients and their families. Gossip is idle talk which foolishly or maliciously spreads rumors or facts. The effects of gossiping are divisive and destructive. Proverbs 11:13 says, "a gossip goes around telling secrets, but those who are trustworthy can keep a confidence."

I get it. Finding out information about others can be fun and entertaining. However, gossiping can be damaging, hurtful, and devastating. Proverbs 16:28 tells us, "A troublemaker plants seeds of strife; gossip separates the best of friends." As Christians, we should act differently from everyone else. When everyone is gossiping and spilling tea about a coworker, what do you do? Do you ask questions for specific details? Do you sit back, say nothing, but still listen? Or, do you remove yourself from the situation? Do you redirect others indulging in juicy gossip?

If we identify ourselves as Christians, our speech and conversations should align with the Word of God. We must be intentional about the conversations we choose to participate in. If what is being said is not fruitful or encouraging, we should remove ourselves from the conversation. 2 Timothy 2:16-17 says this: "Avoid worthless, foolish talk that only leads to more godless behavior. This kind of talk spreads like cancer." Gossip turns people away from God. It will affect your witness and your influence. Even if we don't think what we are saying is harmful or damaging to someone's character, we should still ask ourselves, "Is what I am talking about adding to this person's life and well-being or taking away from it?" Proverbs 4:24 (The Message) says it like this: "Don't talk out of both sides of your mouth; avoid careless banter, white lies, and gossip."

Avoiding gossip may not always be easy, but it is the right choice. First, pray. Ask God to help you. Grace is available to help you do the right thing, even when you feel like it is impossible. Second, make a decision that you will not entertain gossip. Be courageous; choose to walk away when faced with the opportunity to gossip. Next, mind your business. 1 Thessalonians 4:11-12 says, "Make it your goal to live a quiet life, minding your own business and working with your hands, just as we instructed you before. Then people who are not believers will respect the way you live, and you will not need to depend on others." Respect is a result of minding your business, staying away from Talking Tommy, Petty Patty, and Messy Mary.

Dose for the Day

Today, decide NOT to participate in gossip. If you are faced with it, choose to call it out boldly and walk away. God will be pleased with your courageous decision!

Daily Prayer

Dear Heavenly Father,

I thank You and praise You for your grace and mercy, even when I choose to engage in ungodly conversations. Help me to see the harm associated with gossip. Let everything I say be good and helpful, so that my words may be encouraging to everyone who hears them. Allow my words to build people up, and not tear them down. Give me the strength to walk away from gossip instead of tolerating careless chatter. Give me the courage and boldness necessary to call it out in love and kindness. Take control of my lips and keep my lips sealed. Help me to stay silent when issues arise that have nothing to do with me or my work. Your word tells us that this type of talk does not fit our lifestyle and that thanksgiving is our dialect. Help me turn to words of thanksgiving when faced with the temptation of gossip and fruitless talk. Instead of finding fulfillment and satisfaction in gossip, help me to speak words of peace, love, kindness, and faith. In Jesus' Name, Amen.

Scriptural References: Proverbs 11:13; Proverbs 16:28; 2 Timothy 2:16-17; Proverbs 4:24; 1 Thessalonians 4:11-12; Ephesians 4:29; Psalm 141:3

Up For The Challenge

Unlike many other career fields, healthcare changes daily. You never know what you will face when you show up to your job. With that being said, I am sure many, if not all of you can relate to having your share of bad or challenging days. One thing we must realize is that there is no such thing as a job without problems or difficulties. Unless you work with perfect individuals, you will always face challenges at work. John 16:33 tells us, "I have told you these things, so that in Me you may have [perfect] peace and confidence. In the world you have tribulation and trials and distress and frustration; but be of good cheer [take courage; be confident, certain, undaunted]! For I have overcome the world. [I have deprived it of power to harm you and have conquered it for you.]. "

Friends, to be completely honest, I have to constantly renew my mind in this truth. I remember when I began my last travel nurse assignment at a small hospital. I was so excited and looked forward to ending my travel nursing journey on a positive note. By this time, I had been a nurse for about five years. My first day did not go as planned. I had a patient who coded (basically he went into respiratory distress), and I had to transfer him to an intensive care unit ASAP. After that, the charge nurse gave me two more patients. I did not get to eat lunch or make rounds on all of my patients, so I was late giving medications, etc. It was a horrible day. I cried on my way home, questioning whether I forgot to do something. I wondered why I had to have the worst day ever instead of someone else. The next day, I spoke with the nurse manager about everything, and she ensured that I would not get bogged down like that again.

You would think that after five years, I would have learned that challenging days come with the territory of being alive, right? Wrong. Four years later, I began a new career as a nurse practitioner (NP). The transition was a huge challenge for me. On the day I started, the clinic was undergoing training for a new computer program. So, not only did I have to learn how to function as an NP, but I also had to learn how to document with a new system. My second day, I was seeing patients by myself while my supervisor was in training. Oh, did I mention this was during one of the craziest flu seasons in years? Yes, that was a tough time for me. Looking back, I was totally spazzing out, because my boss was only in the next room, readily available for any questions I had. I thought I would waltz in the clinic and my transition would be a cake walk. Unfortunately, I learned the hard way.

I cannot tell you how many times I thought about and actually planned on leaving my job because of the challenges I faced. If those first few months taught me nothing else, they taught me that challenges come with every new season of your life. It does not mean that you are doing anything wrong, nor does it mean that you are not doing what you are supposed to be doing. Like me, you will look back at all of these tough times and realize that God's hand was on you the whole time. Be encouraged! You are more than able to endure every problem that comes your way.

Psalm 46:10 says, "Be still, and know that I am God!" When you feel the sting of a bad day, stop and acknowledge that God is with you. Know that you are never alone. Quitting should not be your first instinct. 1 Thessalonians 5:16-18 says, "Always be joyful. Never stop praying. Be thankful in all circumstances, for this is God's will for you who belong to Christ Jesus." In the midst of the craziness, decide to pray -- not complain. Expect God to move on your behalf. Take the day one minute at a time. Don't look at the clock every 10 minutes – that will only make you feel worse! Problems, challenges, adverse situations, etc. have an expiration date. It will get better. Isaiah 43:2 says it like this, "When you go through deep waters, I will be with you. When you go through rivers of difficulty, you will not drown. When you walk through the fire of oppression, you will not be burned up; the flames will not consume you. " Be encouraged today, knowing that no matter what you may face, God is with you every single step of the way. "No test or temptation that comes your way is beyond the course of what others have had to face. All you need to remember is that God will never let you down; he'll never let you be pushed past your limit; he'll always be there to help you come through it." (1 Corinthians 10:13)

Dose for the Day

Declare this every day, throughout the day: "God loves, me. He is with me and helping me. What may be impossible for others will not be impossible for me. I am well equipped for this. I am called to this job in this season. God has given me the grace to do this. It may seem hard to me, but nothing is too hard for God."

Daily Prayer

Heavenly Father,

I thank You and praise You for Your presence as I start my day. I know that I cannot avoid every difficult situation at work, but I know that You are with me. If I faint in the day of adversity, then my strength is small. Strengthen me in the areas where I am weak. Help me to lean on You and not my emotions. Surround me with Your peace. With You by my side, when all hell breaks loose, I am calm and collected. I know that what I may encounter is temporary. I choose not to focus on the trouble. Instead, I will focus on those things that I cannot see which will produce a glory that will last forever. I choose not to worry or stress myself out today or the days ahead because I know that You will help me regardless of the situation. I give this day to You and lay every person, situation, and conversation in Your hands. In Jesus' Name, Amen.

Scriptural References: John 16:33; Psalm 46:10; 1 Thessalonians 5:16-18; Isaiah 43:2; 1 Corinthians 10:13; Proverbs 24:10; Psalm 27:3, 2 Corinthians 4:17-18; Matthew 6:34

Why Me?

Not only do we experience adversity on our jobs, but life in general. Afflictions, problematic circumstances, and demanding situations are a part of life. Although I personally would love to, there is no avoiding adversity. One concept we all must remember is that when we are faced with it, we actually have to face it. Do not try to avoid it, and do not run from it. You have two choices: stand or be destroyed. 2 Corinthians 4:8-9 says, "We are pressed on every side by troubles, but we are not crushed. We are perplexed, but not driven to despair. We are hunted down, but never abandoned by God. We get knocked down, but we are not destroyed." It is imperative that we do not focus on what is in front of us, but rather look for what we can learn or gain from the experience. When we focus on God's promises, we will not only endure, but thrive in the middle of the trials. Psalm 46:1 tells us that God is our refuge and strength, always ready to help in times of trouble. How comforting and encouraging is it to know that God is always ready to help us.

Transparent moment: Just like everyone else in the entire world, I have had my share of seemingly complicated and impossible situations. However, the most challenging experience happened about two years ago. I was in nurse practitioner school, in the middle of my first semester of clinical rotations. I was working with a physician who had a private practice. His wife was the office manager, and they had a front desk receptionist and a nurse as their only employees. I always got to the office early, so I would always speak to his wife when I arrived, and she would pleasantly return my greeting. Everything seemed to be going well. One day, in the middle of the day, the physician's wife urgently needed to speak with him. They left, and I pulled out a book to study for an upcoming exam. Within five minutes, the physician returned and said, "Miss Danielle, I'm sorry, but you have to leave."

Confused, I responded, "Okay, is everything alright? I am coming back tomorrow for another clinical day, correct?"

He looked at me and said, "No. You cannot work here anymore. You did not do anything wrong. I'm sorry."

Walking out of that office, I was so confused. I had so many questions: "How am I going to finish this semester? I won't be able to graduate on time. I can't pass this class without these clinical hours!" I was literally on the verge of a panic attack. With tears in my eyes, I called my professor. I explained what had just happened and I could tell that she was more worried about me than anything else. She was just as shocked and confused, and told me, "Sweetheart, don't you worry. We will get this handled as soon as possible."

I had no options other than to pray and declare God's

promises over my life and over that situation. I found scriptures and stood firm on the Word. The next day, the physician called me to apologize, and then told me that his wife wanted me gone. Without giving too many details, she attacked my character. She said some pretty hurtful and false things about me. I am not going to lie; I was struggling. I was so angry. However, despite how my emotions were, I continued to pray. Every time I felt myself get angry or upset about what she said, I quoted Isaiah 54:17, which says, "But in that coming day, no weapon turned against you will succeed. You will silence every voice raised up to accuse you." When I was mentally exhausted and drained, I quoted Psalm 138:7, "By your mighty power I can walk through any devastation, and you will keep me alive, reviving me. Your power set me free from the hatred of my enemies." Emotionally, I felt defeated. I had no idea how I was going to finish the semester. I spent all of my free time trying to find another physician to work with. I searched everywhere, leaving voicemails with no follow-up calls, and visiting clinics with denial after denial. I was beginning to become hopeless.

Finally, after about a week and a half, miraculously, someone returned my call and was willing to help me out. Not only that, my school contacted the previous physician's office, and he allowed me to come back. Because of what happened, the school told me that I only had to be at his office once a week. I cannot make this up. God literally stepped in and handled everything. He made things happen that I could not make happen on my own. Luke 18:7-8 says, "So what makes you think God won't step in and work justice for his chosen people, who continue to cry out for help? Won't he stick up for them? I assure you, he will. He will not drag his feet." And guess what? When it was the end of the semester, the physician who "fired" me gave me a PERFECT evaluation, and I ended up making an "A" in the class. No matter how much the enemy tried to bring me down with this adverse situation, I continued to rise with the help of God. Proverbs 24:16 (The Passion Translation) tells us, "For the lovers of God may suffer adversity and stumble seven times, but they will continue to rise over and over again. But the unrighteous are brought down by just one calamity and will never be able to rise again."

There is no such thing as a hopeless situation with God on your side. Whatever you find yourself facing will eventually pass. It won't last forever. Don't quit. Don't give up. Trust God in the midst of it all. Remind yourself of His goodness and His faithfulness to keep yourself encouraged. Overwhelming victory is yours through Christ.

Dose for the Day

Read John 16:33. Write it down on an index card or sticky note and carry it around with you all day. When you are faced with adversity, pull it out and read it. Be encouraged today.

Daily Prayer

Father God,

Thank You for this day. I know that nothing can ever separate me from Your love. I thank You that overwhelming victory is mine through Christ. Help me to change my perspective when adversity comes my way. Help me realize that my endurance, strength of character, and hope of salvation is being developed. Your word tells me that I should cling to my faith in Christ and to keep my conscience clear. Help me not to act out of how I am feeling. Help me to respond in love and grace. Thank You for delivering me from my troubles. You promise to be a strong refuge when trouble comes. You are close to those who trust in You. Thank You for being such a firm foundation.

Help me maintain a joyful disposition in the midst of affliction. Help me to continue to be a witness to others. If anyone is talking about me, trying to damage my character, or slandering my name, I pray that they would feel Your love and that You will heal their hearts. I choose to forgive anyone who offends me. I refuse to hold grudges and become bitter. I choose not to get offended with You either, God. I release all of my cares and give them to You, because You care about me. I thank You that I am victorious and everything I may face will pass soon. In Jesus' Name, Amen.

Scriptural References: 2 Corinthians 4:8-9; Psalm 46:1; Isaiah 54:17; Psalm 138:7; Luke 18:7-8; Proverbs 24:16; Romans 8:37; 1 Timothy 1:19; Psalm 34:17; Nahum 1:7; 1 Peter 5:7

We > Me

The medical field is complex, ever-evolving, and always changing. So much so that, it is nearly impossible to accomplish one task alone. We, as health care professionals, should know more than anyone else that teamwork is essential. I know, I know. Your coworkers get on your last nerve. I understand completely. However, teamwork and encouragement go hand in hand. Teamwork cannot be effective without some form of encouragement. Hebrews 10:24 says, "Let us think of ways to motivate one another to acts of love and good works."

No one can do it alone, and it's okay to admit it, and it's perfectly fine to ask for help. However, this can be difficult, because, in many areas, there is a shortage of workers in healthcare. We see it on the news on a weekly basis. The responsibilities we have doubled, and as a result, we become overwhelmed, stressed, and overworked. It is challenging to be a team player and help others when you are drowning in your tasks. Moses realized the task before him was too big for him to accomplish alone. In Numbers 11, Moses was dealing with a lot of displeased, ungrateful, and complaining people (sound familiar?). He was frustrated, questioning why

God would put him in the position to deal with them. In Numbers 11:14-17, Moses expresses his feelings and frustrations to God. He said, "I can't carry all these people by myself! The load is far too heavy! If this is how you intend to treat me, just go ahead and kill me. Do me a favor and spare me this misery!" Then the Lord said to Moses, "Gather before me seventy men who are recognized as elders and leaders of Israel. Bring them to the Tabernacle to stand there with you. I will come down and talk to you there. I will take some of the Spirit that is upon you, and I will put the Spirit upon them also. They will bear the burden of the people along with you, so you will not have to carry it alone. "

Even in the midst of Moses' frustrations about the seemingly impossible task, God helped him. We can be comforted with this truth, as well. God will send people our way to help us and send us to help others accomplish what needs to be done. That is what teamwork is all about. It has nothing to do with how we feel. Teamwork provides support, builds trust and confidence with your cohorts. When working together, confidence and trust are created among coworkers. You will feel a sense of encouragement and comfort, knowing that you all are in this together.

Additionally, you will learn about each other's strengths and weaknesses when working as a team. For instance, an improvement in customer service will be increased by effective teamwork. You cannot please everyone, but teams that work together can help meet as many needs as possible.

Ecclesiastes 4:9-12 says, "It's better to have a partner than go it alone. Share the work, share the wealth and if one falls down, the other helps, but if there's no one to help, tough! Two in a bed warm each other. Alone, you shiver all night. By yourself you're unprotected. With a friend you can face the worst. Can you round up a third? A three-stranded rope isn't easily snapped."

If you feel like you don't have a good group of coworkers around you, pray. Ask God to send like-minded, hard-working, caring individuals to help you. Trust and believe that He will.

Dose for the Day

Be a team player today. If you see a coworker struggling, be that extra hand. If you are having a hard time, ask God to help you and to send help your way.

Daily Prayer

Heavenly Father,

I pray that today my coworkers and I will work together as one unit. I pray that You would give me and my team wisdom to accomplish all that is set before us. Help us to organize our thoughts. If conflict arises, help us to communicate well with each other so that the problem is resolved quickly. I understand that I cannot do this job alone. Thank You for sending dependent, supportive people my way. Help me to act like a member of the team. I pray for a sense of unity with those who I work with. I speak peace, harmony, and productivity into this day. Help us to bring out the best in each other. Fill this workplace with energy and no weariness. Allow supernatural results to come from us working together. I pray that the goals that we have set will be accomplished in excellence, in a timely manner, without us feeling tired, overwhelmed, or stressed out. In Jesus' Name, Amen.

Scriptural References:

Hebrews 10:24, Numbers 11:14-17, Ecclesiastes 4:9-12, 1 Corinthians 12:21

Forgotten & Frustrated

Some of my favorite movies to watch during Christmas time is the "Home Alone" series. More specifically, the first two movies. It is hilarious to watch little Kevin create witty and genius traps for the infamous robbers who think they can outsmart an 8-year-old kid. It never fails, however, that there is always a short period of time when Kevin feels bad, hurt, and sad that he is spending the holiday alone. His family forgot about him and left him ALL alone. How do you take a family vacation and forget your child or sibling?

Maybe, we have never experienced it like that, but we have all felt forgotten about. Being forgotten or even feeling forgotten about isn't fun. It is hurtful. In healthcare, it's so easy to feel like this. There are so many things that we do for others that go unnoticed. Because our line of work is so "patient or customer focused," we are often overlooked and taken advantage of. This being said, I have some amazing news for you: YOU ARE NOT FORGOTTEN! God has not forgotten about you. He has not overlooked you, and He is not ignoring you. Believe it or not, He sees you. Hagar in the Bible realized this. She was feeling awful about the treatment she was experiencing, but God spoke to her and encouraged her. Genesis 16:13 says, "She answered God by name, praying to the God who spoke to her, "You're the God who sees me! "Yes! He saw me; and then I saw him!"

When the feeling of being forgotten is not dealt with at first thought, self-pity is inevitable. Someone who felt like this and fell into the pit of feeling sorry for himself was David. In Psalm 13:1-6, David says, "Long enough, God—you've ignored me long enough. I've looked at the back of your head long enough. Long enough, I've carried this ton of trouble, lived with a stomach full of pain. Long enough my arrogant enemies have looked down their noses at me. Take a good look at me, God, my God; I want to look life in the eye, so no enemy can get the best of me or laugh when I fall on my face. I've thrown myself headlong into your arms—I'm celebrating your rescue. I'm singing at the top of my lungs, I'm so full of answered prayers."

In Psalm 77:4-14, David says, "You don't let me sleep. I am too distressed even to pray! I think of the good old days, long since ended, when my nights were filled with joyful songs. I search my soul and ponder the difference now. Has the Lord rejected me forever? Will he never again be kind to me? Is his unfailing love gone forever? Have his promises permanently failed? Has God forgotten to be gracious? Has he slammed the door on his compassion? And I said, "This is my fate; the Most High has turned his hand against me." But then I recall all you have done, O Lord; I remember your wonderful deeds of long ago. They are constantly in my thoughts. I cannot stop thinking about your mighty works. O God, your ways are holy. Is there any god as mighty as you? You are the God of great wonders! You demonstrate your awesome power among the nations. "

David feels forgotten by God, rejected, abandoned, ignored, alone, overwhelmed, and depressed, and he's losing sleep because of it. David acknowledges God's goodness towards the end of his pity parties, but questioned God's presence and faithfulness at the beginning. Even in the depressing and sorrowful state David found himself in, he knew in his heart that his current situation did not define God. David knew God was good. Faith and praise will always put everything back into perspective! That is precisely what we must do when we begin to feel like David. Once we make the decision to wholeheartedly trust God—letting go of what we see and how we feel—our perspective becomes clearer, and we begin to see God in a more accurate light.

It is impossible for God to forget about you. Isaiah 49:14-15 says, "But Zion said, "I don't get it. God has left me. My Master has forgotten I even exist. Can a mother forget the infant at her breast, walk away from the baby she bore? But even if mothers forget, I'd never forget you—never."

Feeling like no one notices you or all of the hard work you have put in what you do? Hebrews 6:10 says, "God is not unjust; he will not forget your work and the love you have shown him as you have helped his people and continue to help them." Whenever a thought comes into your mind that says you are insignificant to God, combat those thoughts with God's Word.

2 Corinthians 10:5 tells us, "We demolish arguments and every pretension that sets itself up against the knowledge of God, and we take captive every thought to make it obedient to Christ." Be encouraged today.

Dose for the Day

If you begin to feel overlooked, begin to do like David and remind yourself of God's goodness. Declare: "I am not forgotten. God loves me. I am significant to God. I am always on God's mind. God is always with me."

Daily Prayer

Father God,

Thank You for promising never to forget me. Even if people say I am not significant and choose to overlook me, You said that You see me. Thank You for keeping track of all of my sorrows. You are amazing! You are aware of every hurtful and insensitive thing said to me by others, and You have always been by my side. You promise never to leave me or forsake me. I thank You for the ability to cast my cares on You because You care for me. I choose not to allow the words and actions of others to change my perception of Your faithfulness and love. In Jesus' Name, Amen.

Scriptural References: Genesis 16:13, Psalm 13:1-6, Psalm 77:4-14, Isaiah 49:14-15, Hebrews 6:10, 2 Corinthians 10:5, Psalm 56:8-9, Hebrews 13:6, 1 Peter 5:7

Working vs Productivity

Many of us would describe ourselves as hard workers. Those of us who identify ourselves with working hard cannot relate to just sitting around at work, passing the time by shopping online, chatting on your cell phone, or taking hour-long breaks while staying on the clock. Most of our days are nonstop, with no time for breaks, but are we staying busy just to be busy or are we actually being productive? Busy is defined as being in use; full of activity; foolishly or intrusively active: full of distracting detail. To be productive is to be effective in bringing about yielding results, benefits, or profits. To be fruitful means yielding or producing fruit; conducive to an abundant yield; abundantly productive. See, my friends, there is a difference between being busy and being productive. The result of productivity is a positive result. There is no positive result from being busy. Proverbs 12:11 says, "He who tills his land shall be satisfied with bread, but he who follows worthless pursuits is lacking in sense and is without understanding."

An important concept to remember is that to be productive and fruitful, you must know what you are supposed to do. Take a few minutes and perform a self evaluation. What are your daily tasks, responsibilities, and what is expected of you? If you are not 100% sure, ask your supervisor or someone who knows. Maybe you should take a look at the employee handbook and review your job description. Integrity is a must in order to be productive and fruitful. No internet browsing, shopping, daydreaming, studying, etc. while on the clock. You cannot be productive without integrity. Believe it or not, God places high importance on how we approach work. After all, He is the one you are truly working for. Ephesians 6:5-8 tells us, "Slaves, obey your earthly masters with deep respect and fear. Serve them sincerely as you would serve Christ. Try to please them all the time, not when they are watching you. As slaves of Christ, do the will of God with all your heart. Work with enthusiasm, as though you were working for the Lord rather than for people. Remember that the Lord will reward each one of us for the good we do, whether we are slaves or free."

Additionally, it is impossible to produce fruit without Jesus. John 15:4-5 says, "Remain in me, and I will remain in you. For a branch cannot produce fruit if it is severed from the vine, and you cannot be fruitful unless you remain in me." Fruitfulness is a result of being in Christ and allowing Him to come live in and through us. The key to fruitfulness is not what we can do in our strength, wisdom, or effort. When we abide in Him, we surrender our job, daily tasks and responsibilities totally to Him. God will most definitely do His part. He will help us and enable us to produce fruit, and fruit that yields amazing results. Where we choose to abide will determine the fruit we experience in our lives. Ecclesiastes 9:10 tells us, "Whatever you do, do well.." That should be our daily prayer, that God would enable us to have a productive mindset so that we can do our job well.

Dose for the Day

Make a list of (realistic) work goals and cross them out as you accomplish them. You will feel a sense of productivity at the end of your day. If you do not know what your tasks or responsibilities are, find out and go from there.

Daily Prayer

Father God,

Thank you for this day. I thank you for the opportunity to work. I will not take it for granted. Your word says I should be strong and courageous because my work will be rewarded. I am ready to take on my assignment(s) for this day. Bless the works of my hands and make my efforts successful. I will achieve all that I set to accomplish today because I embrace a productive mindset, as opposed to "busy work." I will see abundant results. Thank you for making me productive and fruitful. Help me to see I am truly working for You rather than men. I declare I operate in integrity and excellence. Thank You for an amazing day. In Jesus' Name, Amen.

Scriptural References: Proverbs 12:11, Ephesians 6:5-8, John 15:4-5, Ecclesiastes 9:10, 2 Chronicles 15:7, Psalm 90:17

DAY TWELVE
Empathy Matters

Like kindness and compassion, empathy is vital in healthcare. Caring for others requires a certain level of empathy. Working for others requires empathy, too. Many times, the people around us are dealing with things we know absolutely nothing about. I am not just talking about patients, either. You, me, our coworkers, supervisors, families, friends, church members—we all need empathy when life becomes tough. Empathy defined is, "the action of understanding, being aware of, being sensitive to, and vicariously experiencing the feelings, thoughts, and experience of another of either the past or present without having the feelings, thoughts, and experience fully communicated in an objectively explicit manner." Empathy is not the same as compassion; similar, but not the same. Empathy means you personally can identify and understand the feelings of another person. Compassion is more like feeling sorry for and expressing your genuine concern for another person.

I am sure we have all been in a situation where we have displayed empathy towards another person, or when we may have needed it ourselves. I'll be the first to admit, sometimes being empathetic is difficult. I can remember one situation in particular quite vividly: the very first time I had to diagnose a patient with a severe disease. What made this circumstance so unfortunate was my patient was a child, a precious, sweet little girl. I had to break the news to her and her mother. I personally could relate because I have family members with this same illness. I remember praying before I went into the patient's room. I knew that I could not do this alone. I was emotional myself and needed a minute to pull myself together. I felt like falling apart because naturally, I knew how her mother would react.

I asked God for more grace to help me. Grace enables us to do the seemingly impossible. 2 Corinthians 1:3-5 tells us, "All praise to God, the Father of our Lord Jesus Christ. God is our merciful Father and the source of all comfort. He comforts us in all our troubles so that we can comfort others. When they are troubled, we will be able to give them the same comfort God has given us." At that moment, God comforted me so I could be there for my patient and her mother. God's grace enables us to do what we cannot do on our own. It's okay to admit to God that you can't do it all; because He already knows.

The best example of empathy is Jesus Christ himself. Hebrews 4:15 says, "This High Priest of ours understands our weaknesses, for he faced all of the same testings we do, yet he did not sin." He understood, sympathized, and related to every single person He encountered. When He sees us struggling, stressed, weary, upset, etc., He is moved with compassion. Matthew 9:36 says, "When he looked out over the crowds, his heart broke, because they were weary and dejected." For those of us working in direct patient care, pray for your patients and their families. Many times, they are dealing with circumstances other than their illnesses. With healthcare changing so much and being so fast-paced, the true essence of genuine care is disappearing. We are so busy running around that we are totally unaware of others' needs. We end up missing out on opportunities to help relieve the sting of pain in others. Empathy is the key that unlocks the door to compassion and kindness. Even when it seems like the situation is too difficult to handle or face, you are graced to display empathy to those who need you.

Dose for the Day

Display empathy to someone in your life who needs it. Remember, you are graced for this!

Daily Prayer

Father God,

Thank You for Your Son, Jesus, who is able to understand me and relate to me in every single area of my life. Thank you for giving me grace to display empathy to those around me. I choose to obey your Word and be happy for those who are happy and to weep with those who are sad or sorrowful. Give me a heart of humility and remove pride from my heart. Help me only to say those things that will support and comfort others. You know what every person I encounter is dealing with, so give me the right words to say. Help me bring encouragement, joy, and peace to their day. You comfort me like a mother comforts her child. Thank you for comforting me so that I may comfort others in their times of need. Help me to be intentional with every word, gesture, and action I do because I represent you. In Jesus' Name, Amen.

Scriptural References: 2 Corinthians 1:3-4, Hebrews 4:15, Matthew 9:36, Romans 12:15, Isaiah 66:13

Favor

Everyone likes to be recognized, right? Who doesn't love a good promotion or raise? I used to always look forward to Nurses' Week when I worked at the hospital. Honestly, it was the only time we felt special. Although we mainly got pens and some cake, it felt good to be appreciated and acknowledged for all of our hard work. God's will is not for us to feel special once a year; He wants us to experience His favor all day, every day! As a child of God, you are already special and favored. Promotion, success, unexpected provision, recognition, and open doors are all apart of God's will for you. Psalm 90:17 says, "And let the beauty and delightfulness and favor of the Lord our God be upon us; confirm and establish the work of our hands—yes, the work of our hands, confirm and establish it. "

There are many examples of God's favor in the Bible. Esther, who risked her life, found favor with the King and became Queen. Joseph was sold into slavery by his brothers, "But the Lord was with Joseph and showed him steadfast love and gave him favor." Jesus had favor with God and man. If you take a second and think about it, you have also been granted favor by God.

I was in my second year of nursing, and the Unit Council on the floor I worked on began coming up with ways to increase employee morale. They eventually came up with an idea where they would nominate an employee on our unit and recognize them as "Associate of the Month." This person was someone who got along well with everyone, worked hard, and exceeded their job expectations. The very first "Associate of the Month" Award was given to yours truly on February 23, 2011. I know the exact date because the certificate is hanging up in my office as a reminder of His favor. To say I was shocked is an understatement. I was not expecting it. I didn't ask for it; I seriously wasn't even thinking about it. I was pleasantly surprised, and the council told me it was an unanimous decision. I have to be honest; it felt good. I knew it was nobody but God. God wants you to stand out; He wants you to be recognized. When you do experience His favor, thank and praise God for it. The things that God can do, we cannot do on our own, or in our strength- so don't try to take credit for it!

Psalm 84:11 tells us "For the Lord God is a Sun and Shield; the Lord bestows [present] grace and favor and [future] glory (honor, splendor, and heavenly bliss)! No good thing will He withhold from those who walk uprightly. " God wants you to experience grace, favor, and glory today and every day. I know it seems like it is difficult to experience this in healthcare, but I am a living witness that God's favor is real! Even in what I thought was the worst job ever, God's favor continued to manifest. The favor of God also brings security. Psalm 30:7 says, "Your favor, O Lord, made me as secure as a mountain. " Because of the favor of God on your life, you don't have to worry about anything! God is not intimidated by anything you are currently experiencing in your life. Revelation 3:8 says, "I know all the things you do, and I have opened a door for you that no one can close." I want you to trust God to completely blow your mind with new opportunities, blessings, promotions, and success. Watch Him do it! "May grace (God's favor) and peace (which is perfect well-being, all necessary good, all spiritual prosperity, and freedom from fears and agitating passions and moral conflicts) be multiplied to you in [the full, personal, precise, and correct] knowledge of God and of Jesus our Lord. "

Dose for the Day

Make these declarations before you begin each day (or night for all of my night shifters):

"I am the righteousness of God, so I am entitled to His favor. The favor of God surrounds me everywhere I go, and in everything I do. I am experiencing God's favor limitlessly. God's favor produces supernatural increase, preferential treatment, promotion, increased assets, changes in policies and rules, and recognition. God affirms the work I do and prospers all that I set my hands to. This day is filled with surprises and divine opportunities. God showers me with unmerited favor. Like Jesus, I have favor with both God and man. I have favor with my coworkers and my supervisors."

Daily Prayer

Heavenly Father,

I praise You for who You are in my life. Thank You for Your kindness and goodness. I thank You for supernatural favor. I don't have to work to obtain favor; You give it freely as a gift. I thank You that I will find favor, and be highly-esteemed in the sight of God and man. You have given me all things pertaining to life and godliness. Help me to succeed. I declare I will experience new opportunities, open doors, provisions, prominence, and recognition. Thank You, God, for working behind the scenes and on my behalf. In Jesus' Name, Amen.

Scriptural References: Psalm 90:17, Genesis 39:21, Psalm 84:11, Psalm 30:7, Revelation 3:8, 1 Peter 1:1-3, Proverbs 3:4; 2 Peter 12:2

WHY WORRY?

Worry. I am pretty sure that this is a common thing we all do at some point in our lives. Maybe some of you are worried about something right now. What exactly is worry? Worry means to afflict with mental distress or agitation; or to feel or experience concern or anxiety. Worry can also be defined as, "a sense of uneasiness and anxiety about the future." Scripture indicates that such anxiety is ultimately grounded in a lack of trust in God and his purposes. If we are completely honest with ourselves, many times, worry is our first response to adverse situations. However, we are not supposed to worry. In fact, we are commanded not to worry. Matthew 6:31-34 tells us, "So don't worry about these things, saying, 'What will we eat? What will we drink? What will we wear?' These things dominate the thoughts of unbelievers, but your heavenly Father already knows all your needs. Seek the Kingdom of God above all else, and live righteously, and he will give you everything you need. "So don't worry about tomorrow, for tomorrow will bring its own worries. Today's trouble is enough for today. "

What exactly is the problem with worry? First, worry is rooted in fear. Second, worry opens the door for the enemy to come in and torment us. Worry and trust are mutually exclusive; meaning we cannot do both at the same time. We must choose. Either worry and be miserable or seek and trust God and live in peace. I once heard someone say, "Worry is like a rocking chair; it gives you something to do but leads you nowhere." Worry accomplishes nothing good. Worrying makes us feel worse.

Additionally, if we allow worry to build up in us, it can adversely affect our physical bodies and our minds. Proverbs 12:25 says, "Worry weighs a person down; an encouraging word cheers a person up. " Only prayer and the Word of God can cure us of worry.

Prayer is not only the anecdote to worry, but it also ushers us into the presence of God. Turn your worries into prayers and allow God to be God over your situation. Philippians 4:6-7 says, "Don't fret or worry. Instead of worrying, pray. Let petitions and praises shape your worries into prayers, letting God know your concerns. Before you know it, a sense of God's wholeness, everything coming together for good, will come and settle you down. It's wonderful what happens when Christ displaces worry at the center of your life."

Additionally, we are instructed to give all of our cares to God. 1 Peter 5:7 tells us, "Casting the whole of your care [all your anxieties, all your worries, all your concerns, once and for all] on Him, for He cares for you affectionately and cares about you watchfully." God desires to help us, but we have a part to play. We must relinquish our desire to control or fix our situation by giving it all to God. Give God all of your concerns, cares, anxieties, and worries, and receive His peace, knowing that He is going to take care of you. "So here's what I've learned through it all: Leave all your cares and anxieties at the feet of the Lord, and measureless grace will strengthen you." (Psalm 55:22)

Dose for the Day

Take a piece of paper or index card, and write down every worry you have. It can be about your job, a difficult decision, family, relationships, finances, etc. During your prayer time, give them to God—once and for all. After that, throw your list of concerns away, and believe that in casting your cares on God, you are now worry-free! Say this aloud: "God has all of my concerns; I am not worried about a thing!"

Daily Prayer

Heavenly Father,

Thank you for being the ultimate source of peace. Thank You for calming my mind. I know that it is not Your will that I worry about anything, no matter how big or small. You are willing to take every care so that I can trust You and enjoy a worry-free life. I cast each of these cares on You and release them out of my hands. I allow You to come into my situation(s) and do what only You can do. I admit that I cannot do this on my own. I need You. God, You are good even when my circumstances are not. Now that I have cast all of my concerns on You, I refuse to worry about anything. Instead, I receive Your peace and grace. I am worry-free. In Jesus' Name! Amen.

Scriptural References: Matthew 6:31-34, Proverbs 12:25, Philippians 4:6-7, 1 Peter 5:7, Psalm 55:22

Check Your Thoughts

The way we think, what we think about, and our thought life, in general, is vital to our outlook on life. Our mind is a battlefield. Admit it. If you are thinking negatively about a situation, doesn't it seem as if it is more magnified and troublesome? As believers, our thoughts are to line up with the truth of God's Word. To do this, our mind must be renewed to His way of thinking. Romans 12:2 says, "Do not be conformed to this world (this age), [fashioned after and adapted to its external, superficial customs], but be transformed (changed) by the [entire] renewal of your mind [by its new ideals and its new attitude], so that you may prove [for yourselves] what is the good and acceptable and perfect will of God, even the thing which is good and acceptable and perfect [in His sight for you]."

We should always make sure that our thoughts line up with the Word of God. Do you ever have ungodly thoughts? Sure, you do. We all do! 2 Corinthians 10:4-5 tells us what to do with those thoughts: "The weapons we fight with are not the weapons of the world. On the contrary, they have divine power to demolish strongholds. We demolish arguments and every pretension that sets itself up against the knowledge of God, and we take captive every thought to make it obedient to Christ." You and only you can control what you allow yourself to think about. Be intentional about how you think. Philippians 4:8 tells us what to think about: "I'd say you'll do best by filling your minds and meditating on things true, noble, reputable, authentic, compelling, gracious—the best, not the worst; the beautiful, not the ugly; things to praise, not things to curse." It is not enough to only think good thoughts. You must combat the negative thoughts with the word of God.

As healthcare professionals, there are so many thoughts we can have. I'm speaking from personal experience, but I have struggled in this area with three types of thoughts, and I'm sure some of you will be able to relate. First, there are contradictory thoughts. These are thoughts that go against God's Word. For example, if someone were to call out sick on a day where the nurses were already short, I would think something like, "I'm going to get so overwhelmed today since she called out sick. I'm not going to have any help, and it's going to be a crazy, horrible day." These thoughts are contradictory, because God tells us, "I will not in any way fail you nor give you up nor leave you without support. [I will] not, [I will] not, [I will] not in any degree leave you helpless nor forsake nor let [you] down (relax My hold on you)! "

Next, I've struggled with thoughts of doubt. These thoughts made me question my ability to do what I needed to do. I would have thoughts like, "I can't do this. I'm not good enough or smart enough to grasp this new information." According to God's Word, however, through Christ, we can do ALL things (Philippians 4:13). Lastly, tormenting thoughts were a struggle for me when I first became a nurse. I would lose sleep at night worrying about my shift the next day. I had thoughts like, "If I do this incorrectly, I could kill someone. I could get fired and lose my license. My future dreams will never be accomplished..." Jeremiah 29:11 tells us, "For I know the plans I have for you," says the Lord. "They are plans for good and not for disaster, to give you a future and a hope."

Romans 8:6 says, "So letting your sinful nature control your mind leads to death. But letting the Spirit control your mind leads to life and peace." To have a healthy thought life, we must allow the Holy Spirit to control our minds. If you meditate on a negative thought long enough, you are going to believe it. What you think will show up in your words, actions, and overall attitude. A mind controlled by our flesh brings mental instability, attacks, worry, fear, torment, anxiety, and depression. Life and peace come as a result of allowing the Holy Spirit to control your mind.

Dose for the Day

Decide every day to think about what you are thinking about. Fill your mind with great thoughts, thoughts that are in line with God's Word. Sift through your current thoughts and get rid of any thought that is contradictory to the truth of God's Word. Get familiar with the scriptures in today's devotional, and recite them throughout the day. Enjoy an amazing and peaceful day!

Daily Prayer

Father God,

Thank You for this day. I declare right now, that I will have a fantastic day. Help me to think about what I am thinking about. Help me to filter through my thoughts and get rid of thoughts that are not like You. I choose to focus on things that I truly desire and want to see. I know that to succeed and prosper, I must meditate (think about) on Your Word. I know that when my mind is on You, I am kept in perfect peace. I have the mind of Christ, and I hold the thoughts, feelings, and purposes of His heart. I choose to think on those things that are true, noble, reputable, authentic, compelling, gracious—the best, not the worst; the beautiful, not the ugly; things to praise, not things to curse. I choose to allow heaven to fill my thoughts, and to not only think about things down here on earth. My thoughts will bring me joy and peace, instead of anxiety and turmoil. Thank You for healing my mind so that my thought life is healthy and in line with Your Word. In Jesus' Name, Amen.

Scriptural References: Romans 12:2, 2 Corinthians 10:4-5, Philippians 4:8, Hebrews 13:5, Philippians 4:13, Jeremiah 29:11, Romans 8:6, Joshua 1:8, Isaiah 26:3, 1 Corinthians 2:16, Colossians 3:1-2

JOY

Would you describe yourself as a happy person? Are you always full of joy? Everyone loves the feeling of pure happiness. However, happiness is experienced when the circumstances of our lives are turning in our favor. Despite contrary beliefs, happiness and joy are not the same, although joy feels like happiness. Rick Warren defines joy as, "the quiet confidence that ultimately everything is going to be alright, and the determined choice to praise God in every situation." Happiness means, "a state of well-being and contentment; a pleasurable or satisfying experience." Unlike happiness, joy is not caused or affected by the events or circumstances in our lives. Happiness flourishes when everything is going great, while joy works best during the hard times.

God desires us to live and enjoy a life full of joy. Even in the midst of difficulty, joy is available to us. Proverbs 15:15 says, "Everything seems to go wrong when you feel weak and depressed. But when you choose to be cheerful, every day will bring you more and more joy and fullness." Although a joyful life is available to us, we must decide to always choose joy, no matter what. 1 Thessalonians 5:16-18 says, "Always be joyful. Never stop praying. Be thankful in all circumstances, for this is God's will for you who belong to Christ Jesus. " Philippians 4:4 tells us, "Be cheerful with joyous celebration in every season of life. Let joy overflow, for you are united with the Anointed One!" Joy is a result of being connected to Christ. No matter what season you are in, even in the midst of adversity, your joy glorifies God. According to Galatians 5:22-23, joy is a result of having the Spirit at work in us: "But the Holy Spirit produces this kind of fruit in our lives: love, joy, peace, patience, kindness, goodness, faithfulness, gentleness, and self-control. There is no law against these things!"

Joy is also related to our obedience. John 15:10-11 says, "If you keep My commandments [if you continue to obey My instructions], you will abide in My love and live on in it, just as I have obeyed My Father's commandments and live on in His love. I have told you these things, that My joy and delight may be in you, and that your joy and gladness may be of full measure and complete and overflowing. " God desires us to live a life that is complete and overflowing with joy! As believers, we have a right to experience and operate in the kind of joy that only comes from God. Ephesians 1:3 says, "All praise to God, the Father of our Lord Jesus Christ, who has blessed us with every spiritual blessing in the heavenly realms because we are united with Christ." We have already been blessed with not one, not two, but EVERY spiritual blessing, just because we are joined with Christ. How amazing is that?!

Operating in this kind of joy affects our physical health and overall well-being. Proverbs 17:22 tells us, "A joyful heart is good medicine, but a crushed spirit dries up the bones. " If you have been feeling kind of 'blah' lately, or just not feeling like yourself, perform a self-checkup and evaluate the level of joy in your life. The strength to overcome your adverse circumstances is not your circumstances changing, it is in your ability to have joy. Nehemiah 8:10 is a scripture that I encourage you to memorize and quote often, especially when you just are not feeling it: "Don't be dejected and sad, for the joy of the Lord is your strength!"

No matter what your day/shift/assignment/situation looks like, choose joy anyway. Trust and believe that God will help you to not only get through it, but to maintain a spirit of joy while doing it!

Dose for the Day

Say this aloud now and throughout your day: "I will not be dejected or sad, because the joy of the Lord is my strength! I choose joy no matter what this day will bring!"

Daily Prayer

Father God,

Thank you for this day. I thank You for the ability to live and enjoy life no matter what I am facing. I pray that today, You will help me to choose joy instead of how my body, mind, and emotions want me to act. Through Your joy, I am strong. Thank You for blessing me with every spiritual blessing. I understand that happiness is contingent on my circumstances, but joy is not. I choose joy simply because You are with me at all times and You are faithful. I trust You to help me enjoy my day despite my circumstances. In Jesus' Name, Amen.

Scriptural References: 1 Thessalonians 5:16-18, Philippians 4:4, Galatians 5:22-23, John 15:11, Ephesians 1:3, Proverbs 17:22, Nehemiah 8:10

What Am I Doing?

You have purpose. God has an amazing plan for your life – even if you do not see or fully understand it. Jeremiah 29:11-13 says, "I know what I'm doing. I have it all planned out – plans to take care of you, not abandon you, plans to give you the future you hope for. When you call on me, when you come and pray to me, I'll listen. When you come looking for me, you'll find me. Yes, when you get serious about finding me and want it more than anything else, I'll make sure you won't be disappointed." God knows how amazing His plans are for us. He desires to care for us and give us the life we desire. Although God has a wonderful plan for us, we have a part to play as well. The verse says that when we call on God, look for Him and find Him, then He will listen. In order for us to experience all that God has for us, we must be intentional about our walk with Him. We also have to be obedient to whatever He tells us. God's will is not automatic. God won't direct your path if you aren't willing to put forth any effort.

Don't know what His will is for your life? Not feeling a sense of purpose? Pray! Seek God and pray for wisdom. Colossians 1:9-11 says, "We ask God to give you complete knowledge of his will and to give you spiritual wisdom and understanding. Then the way you live will always honor and please the Lord, and your lives will produce every kind of good fruit. All the while, you will grow as you learn to know God better and better." God will tell you exactly what He wants you to do. If we set our minds on gaining understanding and wisdom, He'll begin to show you His will. James 1:5-8 tells us, "If you need wisdom, ask our generous God, and he will give it to you. He will not rebuke you for asking. But when you ask him, be sure that your faith is in God alone. Do not waver, for a person with divided loyalty is as unsettled as a wave of the sea that is blown and tossed by the wind. Such people should not expect to receive anything from the Lord. Their loyalty is divided between God and the world, and they are unstable in everything they do." Additionally, do some soul searching. What are you passionate about? What is one thing you would gladly do without pay?

Naturally, people will look to the inventor or creator of a product to find out its purpose. For us, we should look to our Creator, God, to tell us what we were made for. Do not allow ANYONE to make you question your purpose or calling. They did not create you, so they cannot tell you why you were created. I cannot tell you how many times people tried to tell me that I should be doing something totally different. I used to let them get to me, but once I realized who I was and whose I was, I just laughed. Ephesians 2:10 says, "For we are God's masterpiece. He has created us anew in Christ Jesus, so we can do the good things he planned for us long ago." You were created for a purpose and to do good things! Jesus knew His purpose, and He did not back down. He went through a lot. He did not pay attention to the naysayers, because He knew His purpose. John 4:34 says, "Then Jesus explained: "My nourishment comes from doing the will of God, who sent me, and from finishing his work." As we yield to the sovereignty of Christ in every area of our lives, we will come into agreement with His will for us. However, many times, we become impatient.

Ephesians 5:17 advises against this, saying, "Don't act thoughtlessly, but understand what the Lord wants you to do." Practically, this means that we should not apply for jobs out of frustration or impatience, or because you hate your current job. I made that mistake when I was applying for practitioner jobs. I applied for every single job I saw, no matter where it was or what the job required. I was frustrated with where I was working at the time, and no doors were opening for me. So, like many of us do, I decided to do things my way. I went on a few interviews. I finally came to my senses when I realized that doing it my way was not working, and I was becoming even more frustrated.

I began to seek and trust God, and was able to avoid a sketchy job situation that would have left me incredibly miserable. If we would seek God about everything, we could save ourselves a lot of disappointment. Proverbs 19:21 tells us, "We humans keep brainstorming options and plans, but God's purpose prevails."

Author and speaker Stormie Omartan said, "Don't worry if you have doubts about whether you can accomplish what God has called you to do. God always calls us to something greater than ourselves – something bigger than we can accomplish on our own. That is because He wants us to rely on Him." Whenever you have those negative or defeatist thoughts concerning your purpose, declare Isaiah 41:9-10, which states, "You are My servant, I have chosen you and have not cast you away: Fear not, for I am with you, be not dismayed, for I am your God. I will strengthen you, yes, I will help you, I will uphold you with My righteous right hand.'" You are chosen! You are not alone. Not only are you chosen, but God will never take away the gifts or calling He has given you. Romans 11:29 tells us, "For God's gifts and his call can never be withdrawn."

As you continue to seek God about His plan for your life, He will continue to work in you. Philippians 2:13 says, "For God is working in you, giving you the desire and the power to do what pleases him." Wake up every morning with the expectation that the purpose and plan God has for you will be revealed. Isaiah 50:4 says, "Morning by morning he wakens me and opens my understanding to his will." God is always speaking, so we should expect to hear His voice every day.

Dose for the Day

Recite and meditate on these scriptures today:

- Proverbs 16:3: "Roll your works upon the Lord [commit and trust them wholly to Him; He will cause your thoughts to become agreeable to His will, and] so shall your plans be established and succeed. "
- Psalm 32:8: "The Lord says, "I will guide you along the best pathway for your life. I will advise you and watch over you. "
- Isaiah 58:11: "The Lord will guide you continually, giving you water when you are dry and restoring your strength. "

Daily Prayer

Father God,

Thank You for the privilege to come to You anytime I need to. I believe that Your plans for my life are beyond my wildest dreams. Help me to wholeheartedly trust You. Forgive me for paying more attention to distractions and considering those things above what You have already promised me. I know that if I seek You and want You more than any other desire, I will not be disappointed. Instead, I will experience joy, satisfaction, and excitement. Thank You for Your faithfulness to me in every area. Continue to reveal my purpose and Your plans for my life. I cast fear and anxiety out of my life now. You have not given me a spirit of fear, but of power, love, and a sound mind. Thank You for creating me with purpose. I choose to obey You and fulfill every plan You have for me. In Jesus' Name. Amen.

Scriptural References: Jeremiah 29:11-13, Colossians 1:9-11, James 1:5-8, Ephesians 2:10, John 4:34, Ephesians 5:17, Proverbs 19:21, Isaiah 41:9-10, Romans 11:29, Philippians 2:13, Isaiah 50:4, Proverbs 16:3, Psalm 32:8, Isaiah 58:11

Be Unapologetically You

These days, it is so easy to look at other people and use their lives as a way to evaluate ourselves and our lives. Social media allows us to look at someone else's highlight reel and tempts us to question ourselves, or what God has called us to do. Say this aloud with me: "I am enough!" Embrace the fact that you are enough; not because of you, but because of the One living on the inside of you. No matter what has been spoken over you in the past, you are enough. Don't pay attention to what others have to say about you. Psalm 27:1 says, "Light, space, zest—that's God! So, with him on my side I'm fearless, afraid of no one and nothing." You are enough. I am enough. We are enough. This is not a negative or self-centered confession. You are enough not by anything that you have done, but through Christ. Philippians 3:3 says, "We rely on what Christ Jesus has done for us. We put no confidence in human effort..." Your imperfections qualify you to be used by God! Think about it; if you had it all together, you wouldn't need God.

God thinks that you are absolutely amazing. Psalm 139:13-17 gives a beautiful description of how God feels about you: "Oh yes, you shaped me first inside, then out;

you formed me in my mother's womb. I thank you, High God—you're breathtaking! Body and soul, I am marvelously made! I worship in adoration—what a creation! You know me inside and out, you know every bone in my body; You know exactly how I was made, bit by bit, how I was sculpted from nothing into something. Like an open book, you watched me grow from conception to birth; all the stages of my life were spread out before you, the days of my life all prepared before I'd even lived one day. Your thoughts—how rare, how beautiful! God, I'll never comprehend them! I couldn't even begin to count them—any more than I could count the sand of the sea." Ephesians 2:10 says, "For we are God's masterpiece. He has created us anew in Christ Jesus, so we can do the good things he planned for us long ago." God created you. Do you understand how amazing that is? You were created to be fearless and confident. He created your amazing personality and your traits. He created a way to communicate with others effectively. And it's enough! No one can impact others the way you can, simply because they are not you. One of my favorite ministers and authors, Lisa Bevere, said this in her book *Without Rival*: "You actually give people permission to disrespect you when you do not express your true self." BE YOU!

Do not allow rejection, opinions, and the harsh and inconsiderate words and actions of others make you feel as if you are anything other than enough. A few months after starting my new career as an NP, and I was finally beginning to find my niche. I was becoming more confident in my capabilities not only on my job, but I was becoming more confident in myself. Naturally, I am a super bubbly, fun, optimistic person. I know that going to the doctor's office for shots is not the most fun thing (especially for my pediatric patients), and so I feel like that is when my personality and encouraging gift shines the most. One day, I entered my patient's room with a big smile and a warm greeting. The patient's grandmother looked me up and down, appearing to be disgusted by my presence. She rolled her eyes and stuck her nose up in the air like she was the Queen of Neverland. She demanded to see a physician because she "did not drive all this way to see JUST a nurse practitioner."

Can I be transparent? I was angry. I was hurt. I was insulted and beyond offended. She had no idea how hard I had worked to get to that point. She had no idea how passionate I was about the health and well-being of others. Her questioning my ability to look after her 4-year-old granddaughter left me speechless. I quickly left the room in tears. Ultimately, the situation was handled, and they left without seeing anyone. My boss, who is a physician, had my back and supported me.

What do we do when someone questions the very thing God has told us to do? Romans 11:29 is one of my favorite scriptures, and these two translations helped me out greatly during this time. The Message translation says, "God's gifts and God's call are under full warranty—never canceled, never rescinded." The Amplified version says, "For God's gifts and His call are irrevocable. [He never withdraws them when once they are given, and He does not change His mind about those to whom He gives His grace or to whom He sends His call.]" Be encouraged in knowing that God never takes back the gifts He has given. Never allow anyone to make you question your calling, your purpose, or your passions!

Be confident in the God in you. You are enough. You are qualified. You can do it. If you focus on your weaknesses or limitations long enough, you will be intimidated. Philippians 4:13 says, "For I can do everything through Christ, who gives me strength." Be encouraged, friends! There is something inside of you that the world needs.

Dose for the Day

Declare this aloud to start your day: "Regardless of what anyone may think, I am equipped. I am enough. God has qualified me for my purpose and assignments!"

Daily Prayer

Father God,
Thank You for being the Ultimate Creator. There is no reason for me to lack confidence and healthy self-esteem. Help me to realize that I am enough on my job, in my relationships, in my business, and in every area of my life. You called me for such a time as this. Help me not to allow others to plant seeds of doubt in my heart. I realize that there is no reason for me to question my worth or my adequacy. I lack nothing. I am fearless and confident. In Christ, I am enough. In Jesus' Name, Amen.

Scriptural References: Psalm 27:1, Philippians 3:3, Psalm 139:13-18, Ephesians 2:10, Romans 11:29, Philippians 4:13

Idle Hands

I don't know about you, but I live for a day off work. Saturdays are probably one of my favorite days of the week. I greatly enjoy a free Saturday when I have no plans. I can stay in my pajamas all day, and binge watch my favorite shows on Hulu and Netflix. Lazy days are pure bliss. The dictionary defines lazy as, "disinclined to activity or exertion: not energetic or vigorous; encouraging inactivity or indolence; moving slowly: sluggish." That is precisely how I would describe my free Saturdays. Though it is vital to have lazy days, we must not make laziness a habit in our lives. When it comes to our work ethic, lazy is not a word that should be used to describe us.

I don't have many pet peeves, but one of them is watching laziness in action at work. Throughout my career, I have watched coworkers browse and shop on the internet, while I am running around, hungry, tired, and sweating like a madwoman. Working in healthcare, you cannot afford to be lazy. We are servants, and there is nothing positive or beneficial about a lazy servant. It sounds like an oxymoron, to me. To be a servant means to be of use; to give the service and respect due to. You are of no use if you are lazy. Proverbs 16:3 says, "Roll your works upon the Lord [commit and trust them wholly to Him; He will cause your thoughts to become agreeable to His will, and] so shall your plans be established and succeed."

We are supposed to give our work to God, and He will do what He does. However, if we do not work or if we operate in laziness, God has nothing to work with. Romans 12:11-12 tells us, "Never be lazy, but work hard and serve the Lord enthusiastically. Rejoice in our confident hope. Be patient in trouble, and keep on praying." If you struggle with laziness, remember that you are not working for man, but the Lord. Changing your perspective of who you are serving will help you see the bigger picture. In this field, we are in a position to serve others. Healthcare should always be about serving others. In serving others, you are serving God!

Proverbs 10:4 says, "Lazy people are soon poor; hard workers get rich." God desires us to be prosperous. He wants to bless us so that we can bless others. However, you cannot operate in prosperity if you are lazy. Think about it. Do you know of anyone (friend, family member, entertainer, philanthropist, professional athlete, etc.) who is prosperous but does not work? Me neither. Additionally, it is difficult to live the kind of life that God has called us to live if we are lazy. Proverbs 12:27 says, "A lazy life is an empty life, but "early to rise" gets the job done." Another translation reads, "The lazy man does not roast what he took in hunting, but diligence is man's precious possession." If diligence and working hard are traits that will benefit us in life, why not embrace that?

Dose for the Day

Make this declaration: "I am never lazy, but I work hard, and I am diligent in every area of my life. Everything I put my hands to will prosper!"

Daily Prayer

Father God,

Thank You for this day. Thank You for the opportunity to work and serve You. I pray that I do not operate in laziness. If there is an opportunity to be lazy, help me to choose another way to spend my time, whether its helping co-workers or going to my boss to see if there is anything that needs to be done. I pray that You enable the works of my hands so that all of my efforts and hard work will be successful. In Jesus' Name, Amen.

Scriptural References: Proverbs 16:3. Romans 12:11-2, Proverbs 10:4, Proverbs 12:27

Shine!

I do not know anyone who does not enjoy the sunshine. There is nothing better than a perfect sunny day with a nice breeze. What makes sunshine so unique? What does it mean to shine? Shine is defined as having "a bright glowing appearance; to emit rays of light; and to be bright by reflection of light." We as believers should display that bright, glowing appearance -- all of the time. You should display light and not darkness. Matthew 5:14-16 says, "Here's another way to put it: You're here to be light, bringing out the God-colors in the world. God is not a secret to be kept. We're going public with this, as public as a city on a hill. If I make you light-bearers, you don't think I'm going to hide you under a bucket, do you? I'm putting you on a light stand. Now that I've put you there on a hilltop, on a light stand—shine! Keep open house; be generous with your lives. By opening up to others, you'll prompt people to open up with God, this generous Father in heaven."

What is light? Light is defined as something that makes vision possible; inner light, enlightenment, truth; to ignite something." Light involves the removal of darkness. 1 John 1:5 tells us, "God is light, and there is no darkness in him at all." John 8:12 says, "Jesus spoke to the people once more and said, "I am the light of the world. If you follow me, you won't have to walk in darkness, because you will have the light that leads to life."

Guess what? As Christians, believers, and followers of Christ, we are His representatives. That being said, we should shine as bright lights as well – at work, at home, at church, during sporting events, in Target, and Starbucks. Our goal as representatives is to give people Jesus. Colossians 3:17 says, "And whatever you do or say, do it as a representative of the Lord Jesus, giving thanks through him to God the Father. "

Even in the midst of frustrations, we represent Christ, and we need to function as such. Do not allow life to dim your light. Ephesians 5:8-9 says, "For once you were full of darkness, but now you have light from the Lord. So live as people of light! For this light within you produces only what is good and right and true. " Satan, our enemy, is terrified of you, especially when your light is shining brightly for all of the world to see. He is terrified of your gift. He is terrified of you pursuing purpose. When you allow your light to shine, he has nowhere to go. Light and darkness cannot coexist. You are a reminder to him that he is absolutely powerless. The light of Christ inside of you is a constant reminder that he is unable to be light. Philippians 2:5 tells us that we should be "shining like bright lights in a world full of crooked and perverse people."

Other than being the amazing person you are, there are other ways to shine, especially at work. Working in healthcare, you may find it challenging to display light.

Stress, ungrateful and demanding patients/family members, overwhelming demands, you name it—the enemy will try and use these circumstances to keep you from doing what you have been called to do: shine brightly! Display love and kindness. Be yourself. More than anything, copy Jesus. He is the perfect example of light. Here are some simple ideas:

- Help an overwhelmed coworker.
- Pray for someone who is having a bad day.
- Bake cookies or bring doughnuts and coffee for everybody.
- Compliment someone.
- Use your gift to assist someone else.
- Write someone an encouraging note/scripture and tape it to their workstation.

Dose for the Day

Implement one of the ideas given in the devotional or come up with your own idea to display light and shine at work.

Daily Prayer

Father God,

Thank you for a new day. I am grateful that your mercies are new every morning. As I begin my day, I confess that I need you to help me. Help me to allow my light to shine brightly before every person I encounter today. I pray that every person I interact today feels Your love. I am determined to represent You well. Even if I become frustrated or experience challenges, I pray that Your light will shine through me so that You will get all of the glory. I know that I cannot do it alone. Allow my speech and my actions to line up with what I say I believe. I choose to think before I speak, and I pray that You will tell me who I need to help, talk to, encourage, or pray for. I pray specifically for every person with whom I will be interacting and conversing with today. Today will be a day full of life and light. I declare that I will have a great day. In Jesus' Name, Amen.

Scriptural References: Matthew 5:14-16, 1 John 1:5, John 8:12, Colossians 3:17, Ephesians 5:8-9, Philippians 2:15

Make Time

When was the last time you had "me time?" When was the last time you enabled the "Do Not Disturb" feature on your phone? When was the last time you had a day when you did nothing productive, but just rested and relaxed? If it was more than one week ago, my friend, that's a problem. We should incorporate "me time" at least once a week. You need to take care of you. Self-care is important and necessary. We as healthcare professionals spend our days and nights serving and pouring into the lives of others, making sure that their needs are being met. Our focus is always customer or patient-centered. Sometimes, those people are not appreciative, but demanding, rude, and stressful. They have no idea the blood, sweat, and tears you have gone through to help them. I have had MANY days when my drive home from work consisted of me sobbing because the days were so rough. I have had days when I felt utterly depleted and exhausted. When you have days like that, and you do not give yourself time to de-stress and release, it will negatively affect you. It'll show up in your physical body, emotions, and/or your mental state.

Why is incorporating this concept of "me time" and self-care so critical? I'm sure that you all are very aware of the mental health issues that have been making headlines. Statistics show that those working in healthcare are more likely to commit suicide. That's a tough reality to accept. Let's be honest. In my opinion, we have some of the hardest jobs on the planet. We are faced with unrealistic expectations, stress, burnout, excessive pressure to meet deadlines, overworked, and understaffed.

If you are feeling worn out, tired, or depleted, allow Matthew 11:28-30 to encourage you: "Come to Me, all you who labor and are heavy-laden and overburdened, and I will cause you to rest. [I will ease and relieve and refresh your souls.] Take My yoke upon you and learn of Me, for I am gentle (meek) and humble (lowly) in heart, and you will find rest (relief and ease and refreshment and recreation and blessed quiet) for your souls. [Jer. 6:16.] For My yoke is wholesome (useful, good—not harsh, hard, sharp, or pressing, but comfortable, gracious, and pleasant), and My burden is light and easy to be borne. "

Another translation says it like this: "Are you tired? Worn out? Burned out on religion? Come to me. Get away with me and you'll recover your life. I'll show you how to take a real rest. Walk with me and work with me—watch how I do it. Learn the unforced rhythms of grace. I won't lay anything heavy or ill-fitting on you. Keep company with me and you'll learn to live freely and lightly." It is not God's will for you to feel overwhelmed and worn out. Allow Him to replenish your strength and peace of mind. Rest is God's will for you. Make it a habit to pray for your mental health. Pray against anxiety, panic attacks, depression, and suicidal thoughts. 2 Corinthians 10:5 says, "We demolish arguments and every pretension that sets itself up against the knowledge of God, and we take captive every thought to make it obedient to Christ."

Do not feel bad for taking time out for you. Leave work at work. You cannot rest and work at the same time. I know, it is easier said than done, but you need that time not only for your health and well-being but for your life. God himself even rested after He created the earth. Genesis 2:2 says, "By the seventh day God had finished the work he had been doing; so on the seventh day he rested from all his work." Hebrews 4:9-11 tells us, "So there is a special rest still waiting for the people of God. For all who have entered into God's rest have rested from their labors, just as God did after creating the world. So let us do our best to enter that rest." God instructs and wants you to rest. Being overwhelmed, stressed, worked up, etc.—that opens the door to negative thoughts. He wants us to enjoy the life that He has blessed us with.

A misconception of "me time" or self-care is that you have to spend money. False. I have "staycations" all of the time. A staycation is basically when you have a vacation at home and do things that you enjoy. You can watch your favorite movie, take a nap, read a book, take a walk in the park, workout, etc. If you want to spend money, ladies may enjoy a manicure/pedicure/spa day, and men may enjoy going to a basketball or football game. Whatever you decide to do, make time for you. Your emotional, physical, mental, and spiritual well-being is worth it.

If any of you are struggling in this area and have dealt with or are currently experiencing suicidal thoughts, you are not alone. I am praying for you. God loves you unconditionally. Please, talk to someone. The National Suicide Prevention Hotline is available 24/7: 1-800-273-8255

Dose for the Day

Plan your next "me time" appointment and mark it on your calendar.

Daily Prayer

Heavenly Father,

Thank You for being my safe haven and strong tower. When I feel tired, stressed, or overwhelmed, I know that I can come to You for strength. Anxiety, depression, panic attacks, isolation, and suicidal thoughts are not apart of me. I pray for the ability to care for myself while caring for others. I give You my cares and receive Your relief, rest, and refreshing peace. I thank You that I am not alone. I pray that as I pour into others You will pour back into me. Give me creative and witty ideas for my self-care days. I choose to love myself enough to take time out for me. I pray that when I sleep at night, my sleep will be sweet. Everything that I am concerned or stressed about, I give to You. I refuse to worry about it any longer. In Jesus' Name, Amen.

Scriptural References:

Matthew 11:28-30, 2 Corinthians 10:5, Genesis 2:2, Hebrews 4:9-11

Graced for This

Do you ever look at your life and wonder how you have made it this far? God is amazing and has been so good to us all, no doubt. We are here because of His grace. 1 Corinthians 15:10 says, "But because God was so gracious, so very generous, here I am." Have you ever looked at the assignment or challenge before you and doubted your ability to do it? Sure, you have, we all have. The good news is, you are not alone, and you have access to His grace. Not only that, you are graced for whatever it is that you are doing. Grace is God's unmerited favor; His ability added to your ability. Empowerment and enablement. Power. Divine help. Grace causes you to do more than your natural ability alone. Guess what? You are already equipped with grace. Ephesians 1:3 says, "All praise to God, the Father of our Lord Jesus Christ, who has blessed us with every spiritual blessing in the heavenly realms because we are united with Christ." You are already blessed! Grace, peace, joy, love—it has already been given to you. You just have to receive it. You have free access to every blessing, and that includes grace!

Grace is real. It is God's grace that gives you the ability to be the fantastic nurse, social worker, receptionist, pharmacist, nursing assistant, phlebotomist, physician, medical biller, pharmacy technician, etc.! Romans 12:6 says, "In his grace, God has given us different gifts for doing certain things well." What you do, it is not just a job. It is your assignment in this season. When you find yourself stressed and frustrated, it could be because you are trying to do it in your strength. The awesome thing about grace is that we cannot do anything to earn it. Grace is a gift from God. How mind-blowing is that?

Romans 11:6 tells us, "And since it is through God's kindness, then it is not by their good works. For in that case, God's grace would not be what it really is—free and undeserved. " Grace is God doing something for us that we do not deserve and cannot earn; We do not qualify for grace.

1 Corinthians 12:9-10 says, "My grace is enough; it's all you need. My strength comes into its own in your weakness. Once I heard that, I was glad to let it happen. I quit focusing on the handicap and began appreciating the gift. It was a case of Christ's strength moving in on my weakness. Now I take limitations in stride, and with good cheer, these limitations that cut me down to size—abuse, accidents, opposition, bad breaks. I just let Christ take over! And so the weaker I get, the stronger I become." You see, my friend, the power of God's grace is not seen until we fully acknowledge our weakness and limitations. The moment you realize how helpless you are is the moment when you are ready to receive grace and realize that His grace is more than enough. You must put our total trust in Him. Be humble enough to admit that you

cannot do it alone. If you come to a situation that seems hopeless, do what you can and pray. Pray and invite God into your situation. Pray for more grace and supernatural ability to do whatever it is that you need to do. God will most definitely step in and do what you cannot. Hebrews 4:15-16 tells us, "This High Priest of ours understands our weaknesses, for he faced all of the same testings we do, yet he did not sin. So let us come boldly to the throne of our gracious God. There we will receive his mercy, and we will find grace to help us when we need it most. "Not only is He readily available for us to come to Him, But He also relates to us. He understands our weakness.

You are graced, my friend. You are graced for every season you find yourself in. Because of this grace, you can do the seemingly impossible.

Dose for the Day

Make these declarations:
- I am graced.
- His grace is enough for me.
- I have the capacity to operate at a supernatural level
- because of grace.
- I can boldly receive grace from Jesus, whenever I need it.
- His power works best in my weaknesses.
- I daily receive His grace to help me during the day, all day.
- His grace is powerful.
- His grace is unmerited.
- I am empowered and enabled by His grace.

Daily Prayer

Father God,

Thank You for grace. I thank You that through Christ and what He did for me, I have been blessed with every spiritual blessing. Grace is a spiritual blessing, and I receive it now. I pray for an outpouring of Your grace. Give me more grace to do what You are instructing me to do. Give me more grace for my assignment. Give me more grace to be content in this season of my life. You have given me a gift, and I choose to fully operate in that so that Your grace surrounds me in everything I do. I am thankful that You understand my weaknesses. I thank You that Your strength is made perfect in my weakness. Your grace is more than enough, powerful, real, and divine. Help me to extend grace to others as You have done for me. Help me to be kind and respond gracefully. In Jesus' Name, Amen.

Scriptural References: 1 Corinthians 15:10, Ephesians 1:3, Romans 12:6, Romans 11:6, 2 Corinthians 12:9-10, Hebrews 4:15-16

Ultimate Boss

What are some qualities of a good boss? In my personal opinion, the perfect boss would be a person who is honest, compassionate, understanding, readily available to help, gracious, an excellent communicator, consistent, knowledgeable, and who keeps his/her word. Most of us do not have all of these characteristics in our boss (and if you do, consider yourself blessed!). However, as believers, we do not work for man. God is our ultimate boss, and He is perfect. Colossians 3:22-24 tells us, "Servants, do what you're told by your earthly masters. And don't just do the minimum that will get you by. Do your best. Work from the heart for your real Master, for God, confident that you'll get paid in full when you come into your inheritance. Keep in mind always that the ultimate Master you're serving is Christ." If you find yourself frustrated with work or those in authority over you, remember who you are truly working for.

Although our ultimate boss is Christ, we still have a responsibility and will be held accountable for how we work and how we treat our natural bosses. Romans 12:11 tells us, "Never be lazy, but work hard and serve the Lord enthusiastically." We are actually instruct-ed to pray for those in authority. 1 Timothy 2:2 says, "Pray this way for kings and all who are in authority so that we can live peaceful and quiet lives marked by godliness and dignity." No matter how you may feel about them, pray for them. Pray that God would help them make wise decisions. Prayer works. Do you need a day off and your boss won't budge? Do you need to change your schedule so you can make it to your son's soccer games? Pray. Pray for God to change their hearts towards you. Proverbs 21:1 says, "The king's heart is like a stream of water directed by the Lord; he guides it wherever he pleases. "

God is interested in the details of your life. Big or small, significant, or insignificant. He delights in every single detail. He cares about the things that you care about. Psalm 37:23 says, "The Lord directs the steps of the godly. He delights in every detail of their lives. " That's just the kind of God He is. He is the perfect boss.

He is always available and ready to help you. Hebrews 13:5-6 says, "for He [God] Himself has said, I will not in any way fail you nor give you up nor leave you without support. [I will] not, [I will] not, [I will] not in any degree leave you helpless nor forsake nor let [you] down (relax My hold on you)! [Assuredly not!] So we take comfort and are encouraged and confidently and boldly say, The Lord is my Helper; I will not be seized with alarm [I will not fear or dread or be terrified]. What can man do to me?"

God is presently working in you. Philippians 2:13 tells us, "[Not in your own strength] for it is God Who is all the while effectually at work in you [energizing and creating in you the power and desire], both to will and to work for His good pleasure and satisfaction and delight. "

He is the Creator. He is all-knowing and all-powerful. He never gets tired. He is strength. There is nothing that He does not know or is not aware of. Isaiah 40:28-29 says, "Have you not known? Have you not heard? The everlasting God, the Lord, the Creator of the ends of the earth, does not faint or grow weary; there is no searching of His understanding. He gives power to the faint and weary, and to him who has no might He increases strength [causing it to multiply and making it to abound]."

He cannot lie nor does He ever change His mind. Numbers 23:19 tells us, "God is not a man, so he does not lie. He is not human, so he does not change his mind. Has He ever spoken and failed to act? Has he ever promised and not carried it through? " He keeps His word. He is consistent. He does not change, nor does he change the promises He has made to us. Psalm 89:34 says, "No, I will not break my covenant; I will not take back a single word I said."

Dose for the Day

Meditate on one of the scriptures in today's devotional.

Daily Prayer

Heavenly Father,

Thank You for being the ultimate boss. Thank You for being the perfect boss. You are loving, understanding, readily available, consistent, honest, compassionate, and helpful. I pray for my earthly supervisor/boss. I pray that You would do a mighty work in his/her heart. I pray for favor and supernatural grace in dealing with them. Any and every desire I have that requires their approval, I bring before You now. Your word says that You, Lord, will fight for me and I will not have to lift a finger. Help me to realize that You are interested in all of the details of my life. I choose to involve and include You in every area, big or small. Help me to trust that You are a good God, even when I feel as though my earthly boss is not. I choose to pray for them, without gossiping or complaining about them. In Jesus' Name, Amen.

Scriptural References: Colossians 3:22-24, Romans 12:11, 1 Timothy 2:2, Proverbs 21:1, Psalm 37:23, Philippians 2:13, Isaiah 40:28-29, Numbers 23:19, Psalm 89:34, Ezekiel 14:13-14

UGH!

Dread. I am sure that word describes a feeling you have had before, or are currently experiencing. Dread is "great fear especially in the face of impending evil extreme uneasiness in the face of a disagreeable prospect; to be apprehensive or fearful." In simple terms, dread is a form of fear. Dread, when it is not properly dealt with, can lead to anxiety and depression. The enemy uses dread to rob you of the peace and joy that Jesus sacrificed His life for. Not only that, dread is an indication that we are not walking in the reality of God's love for us. You were not created to live a life full of dread. Do you look forward to every day? In expectancy? Do you experience dread every day?

I remember when I was a new nurse, out of school for about six months. This should have been one of the best seasons of my life; however, I was dealing with dread. I could not enjoy my days off of work because I was so worried about what my next day at work would look like. I would think thoughts like, "How many patients am I going to have? Are we going to be fully and adequately staffed? Will I have to float to another floor that I am not familiar with? Will I have to start an IV or administer a blood transfusion?" I was 22 years old, and yet I was going to bed at 5 pm because I had trouble sleeping. I would lay in bed for hours before finally dozing off. My mind would race and my stomach would ache. I cried myself to sleep so many nights. I would stress thinking about what I would possibly face the next day. The days that I worked, I would stress out at 6:45 am about what 5:00 pm would look like.

I remember I called my parents to talk to them, and my dad told me to pray about it. He also encouraged me to avoid looking at the whole day but to take it hour by hour, minute by minute. He encouraged me to find scriptures specific to my situation and begin to declare them over my life daily. That's exactly what I did. I found quite a few, and to this day, these are some of my favorite scriptures:

Isaiah 26:3 says, "You will keep in perfect peace all who trust in you, all whose thoughts are fixed on you! " As long as your focus is on Him and not what you are dreading, God will keep you in perfect peace.

Psalm 29:11 tells us that "The Lord gives his people strength. The Lord blesses them with peace." Not only are we blessed with strength, to endure whatever we dread, but we are promised peace.

Psalm 4:8 says, "In peace I will both lie down and sleep, for You, Lord, alone make me dwell in safety and confident trust. " Since I had so much trouble sleeping, this was the perfect scripture for me to stand on and declare before I went to bed!

Psalm 112:7 says, "They do not fear bad news; they confidently trust the Lord to care for them. " I had to pray and ask God to help me change my thoughts and perspective. My thought life did not align with God's desires for my life. I always anticipated the worst. God helped me understand that even if things were not perfect, I could trust Him to help me and take care of me through it all! It is possible to enjoy God even in the midst of our unpleasant circumstances (including our jobs!).

Philippians 4:6-7 tells us, "Don't worry about anything; instead, pray about everything. Tell God what you need, and thank him for all he has done. Then you will experience God's peace, which exceeds anything we can understand. His peace will guard your hearts and minds as you live in Christ Jesus. "

Whatever you are currently dreading, take it to God. Exchange that toxic dread for His unexplainable peace.

Dose for the Day

Say this aloud: "God is with me always. I can give Him all of my cares, concerns, and dreadful thoughts. God is my helper. He gives me strength and peace. I receive His perfect peace and choose to operate in peace. No more dreadful thinking!"

Daily Prayer

Father God,

Thank You for always being near. I am so incredibly grateful to Jesus for taking care of every fear, sense of dread, and anxiety on the cross. I know that dread is not Your will for my life. I pray that as I focus on You and Your promises, Your peace will consume every part of me. Help me to find a healthy outlet, whether it be exercising, taking a walk in the park, or taking up another hobby. I pray that when I sleep at night, my sleep will be sweet and my thoughts will be pure and lovely. I exchange dread for peace and joy. In Jesus' Name, Amen.

Scriptural References: Isaiah 26:3, Psalm 29:11, Psalm 4:8, Psalm 112:7, Philippians 4:6-7

Scared Straight

Being scared is no fun. Similar to faith, fear is released by the words that we speak. When we operate in fear, we say things that are contrary to what God says in His Word. When we operate in fear, it is tough to follow God. Fear paralyzes us to the point that we are not free to follow God. Fear hinders us from fully trusting Him, which is why we cannot operate in fear and faith at the same time. Fear tells us what we cannot do, cannot have, and who we cannot be.

2 Timothy 1:7 says, "For God did not give us a spirit of timidity (of cowardice, of craven and cringing and fawning fear), but [He has given us a spirit] of power and of love and of calm and well-balanced mind and discipline and self-control. " Fear does not come from God. He loves us, and His love is perfect. 1 John 4:17-18 tells us, "There is no fear in love [dread does not exist], but full-grown (complete, perfect) love turns fear out of doors and expels every trace of terror! For fear brings with it the thought of punishment, and [so] he who is afraid has not reached the full maturity of love [is not yet grown into love's complete perfection]. " Once you have a revelation of how perfect His love is toward you, fear will not overtake you. You

have no reason to fear. Even if you "feel" fear, don't act on it. Remind yourself and daily renew your mind to His unconditional and perfect love. Make praise your initial response to fear. Do not allow fear to stop your dreams, goals, or whatever you are believing God for. God is bigger and greater than all of your fears.

There was a time in the Bible when the disciples experienced fear. John 6:16-21 describes how they were in a boat during a storm and saw Jesus walking on the water towards them, and they were afraid. John 6:19-21 says, "They had rowed three or four miles when suddenly they saw Jesus walking on water toward the boat. They were terrified, but he called out to them, "Don't be afraid. I am here!" Then they were eager to let him in the boat, and immediately they arrived at their destination!" If we catch the revelation that He is always with us, the sooner we will see changes in our lives. When we operate in fear, it seems to prolong the process of getting to where we want to be, because our focus is off. We tend to focus on ourselves, our situations, and our jobs (or lack thereof), instead of focusing on the only One who can change our situation!

Fun fact: "Fear not"/ "Don't be afraid" are said over 300 times in the Bible. We have to make a conscious decision to daily walk in fearlessness, no matter what! Isaiah 41:10 &13 says, "Don't panic. I'm with you. There's no need to fear for I'm your God. I'll give you strength. I'll help you. I'll hold you steady, keep a firm grip on you.. For I the Lord your God hold your right hand; I am the Lord, Who says to you, Fear not; I will help you! " Deuteronomy 31:6 says, "So be strong and courageous! Do not be afraid and do not panic before them. For the Lord your God will personally go ahead of you. He will neither fail you nor abandon you. " I do not think that if living a fearless life was impossible, God would continually instruct us not to be afraid. He is with you, always. He has a strong grip on you, and He will never let go!

Psalm 34:4 says, "I prayed to the Lord, and he answered me. He freed me from all my fears." Another translation says it like this: "God met me more than halfway, he freed me from my anxious fears." Psalm 56:3-4 says, "But when I am afraid, I will put my trust in you. I praise God for what he has promised. I trust in God, so why should I be afraid? What can mere mortals do to me?" Whatever you are currently in fear of, trust that God will deliver you and help you to overcome it. Pray and remind God of His promises, and believe that fear will no longer be a part of you, no matter the situation. Jeremiah 32:27 says, "Stay alert! I am God, the God of everything living. Is there anything I can't do?" Nothing is too hard for God, not even your deepest and greatest fear(s). Trust in Him, His promises, and unconditional love for you and fear no more!

Dose for the Day

Take a moment and think about your fears. Pray and ask God to deliver you from each and every one. Make this declaration: "I will not live in fear. I am fearless!"

Daily Prayer

Father God,

I thank You for Your love. Your perfect and unconditional love. I understand that because of this love, there is absolutely no reason to fear. Give me the grace to fully receive Your perfect love so that fear is not apart of me. Thank You for all of Your promises of Your constant presence in my life. With You on and by my side, fear has no place. Thank You for delivering me from every single fear. I choose to trust You, no matter what I feel, think, or see. I will be strong and courageous and refuse to be cowardly and timid. I choose to embrace my God-given confidence because I have the most powerful One on my side. In Jesus' Name, Amen.

Scriptural References: 1 Timothy 1:7, 1 John 4:18, John 6:19-21, Isaiah 41:10, Isaiah 41:13, Deuteronomy 31:6, Psalm 34:4, Psalm 56:3-4, Jeremiah 32:27

The Best Conversation

Take a moment and think about the most recent pleasant conversation you have had. Maybe you were talking to a family member, your spouse, coworker, or a very close friend. What was it about the conversation that made it so good? Was it the content, the enthusiasm, or maybe it was the advice that was exchanged? A good conversation is one that is a two-way street—involving both talking and listening. Contrary to popular belief, the absolute best conversations are the ones when we talk to God. That is the foundation of prayer.

Prayer is essential to our lives. Prayer should be like breathing, something that we do continually, but often unconsciously. 1 Thessalonians 5:16-17 says, "Always be joyful. Never stop praying." People have made prayer so complicated. In actuality, it is quite simple. You can pray to God about anything. You can converse with God about anything and everything. Don't understand something on your job? Pray. Worried about a bad situation? Pray. Prayer is the anecdote to worry. Philippians 4:6-7 says, "Don't fret or worry. Instead of worrying, pray. Let petitions and praises shape your worries into prayers, letting God know your concerns. Before you know it, a sense of

God's wholeness, everything coming together for good, will come and settle you down. It's wonderful what happens when Christ displaces worry at the center of your life.." Prayer is a sign of humility. It is basically giving up control of the situation and placing it into His hands. Prayer should be your first response and not your last resort. Stop being so concerned about what it will sound like. Stop comparing your prayers with others!

Why pray? Prayer reveals strategies, divine instructions, and brings peace to our situations. Prayer is what aligns our lives with God's will. Prayer is the advantage that we have over adversity. Colossians 4:2 tells us, "Devote yourselves to prayer with an alert mind and a thankful heart.." We should have a life that is devoted to prayer. Prayer is a lifestyle, not an event. Ephesians 6:18 says, "Pray in the Spirit at all times and on every occasion. Stay alert and be persistent in your prayers for all believers everywhere." Pray on every occasion—before your start your day, during tough and overwhelming days at work, pray for your patients, boss, and everyone who you will be interacting with during the day, pray even when you are feeling great. Remember to pray for others, too; your prayer life should not be all about you.

James 5:16 tells us that "the earnest prayer of a righteous person has great power and produces wonderful results." When you pray, you should expect immediate results! When you pray, you should remind God of what His Word says. Find scriptures that line up with what you are praying for. When you pray the scriptures, you are praying God's perfect will. Put Him in remembrance of

His promises. Tell Him that you are in expectation that it will come to pass and continue to thank Him for it. 1 John 5:14-15 says, "This is the confidence we have in approaching God: that if we ask anything according to his will, he hears us. And if we know that he hears us— whatever we ask—we know that we have what we asked of him. " Know that when you pray, He hears you. Psalm 145:18 tells us, "God's there, listening for all who pray, for all who pray and mean it." He wants to hear from you. Commit to praying with passion and persistence, trusting that whatever you are praying for will come in His perfect timing, in His perfect way.

Dose for the Day

Meditate on this scripture today:

Ephesians 6:18: "In the same way, prayer is essential in this ongoing warfare. Pray hard and long. Pray for your brothers and sisters. Keep your eyes open. Keep each other's spirits up so that no one falls behind or drops out."

Daily Prayer

Heavenly Father,

Thank you for being such a good Father. Thank You for the privilege we have to boldly and freely access you through prayer. I know that prayer ushers me into Your presence. Thank You for the promises in Your Word that You have and are still bringing to pass. It is so amazing just to be able to talk to You, even when I don't' need anything. Your Word says that when I feel defeated, I can cry out to You and You will deliver me. I pray for the day ahead of me. I pray for the spirit of wisdom and revelation, spiritual insight and understanding. Your Word says that if I ask, that it will be given to me liberally. Thank You for those times when I don't even know what to pray, Your Word says that the Holy Spirit will intercede for me. Thank You for all that You have blessed me with thus far. I specifically pray for (call out those things that you are praying for), and I trust that You will bring these things to pass. In Jesus' Name, Amen.

Scriptural References: 1 Thessalonians 5:16-17, Philippians 4:6-7, Colossians 4:2, Ephesians 6:18, James 5:16, Psalm 145:18, Psalm 34:6

Remember the Time

Have you ever found yourself in a funk? Have you ever had those days when you feel 'blah?' Do you ever have those days when you are just going through the motions, and not excited about anything? I'm sure many of us have had those days where we find ourselves frustrated, discouraged, and disappointed because nothing ever seems to be working for us. Whenever you start to feel like this, change your thoughts and begin to think about God's faithfulness in the past. Faithful is not just a character trait of God, it is who He is. 2 Timothy 2:13 says, "If we are unfaithful, he remains faithful, for he cannot deny who he is. " No matter where you find yourself in life, begin to recount God's blessings and faithfulness towards you. There is no one like Him. This will not only encourage you, but it will build your faith, as well.

In Psalm 77:10-14, David was going through a very difficult time in his life. He began to question God's presence and His nature. Sound familiar? Whenever we are going through adversity, it feels like we are all alone. David was all in his feelings and he had to stop himself. He changed his perspective. Psalm 77:11-12 says, "But then I recall all you have done, O Lord; I remember your wonderful deeds of long ago. They are constantly in my thoughts. I cannot stop thinking about your mighty works. " He began to ponder on the goodness of God, listing specific examples of how God came through for him in the past. He reminded himself of God's faithfulness in his own life.

When you begin to question His nature, remind yourself of His faithfulness. That is one reason why I believe journaling is so important. Those days when I am feeling 'blah,' I pull my journals out and just read all about what God has done in my life thus far. You must go back and remember those times when God performed miracles on your behalf. You must remember those times when His favor surrounded you and helped you when you did not see a way out. You must remember those times when He made things happen that seemed humanly impossible. You have to learn to encourage yourself with past victories and answered prayers.

Psalm 40:5 says, "O Lord my God, you have performed many wonders for us. Your plans for us are too numerous to list. You have no equal. If I tried to recite all your wonderful deeds, I would never come to the end of them. " There is no one like Him. He is God. Equal means to be the same in quantity or value. There is no one as great and mighty, compassionate and loving as God. He is not like man. He's consistently faithful. Just like He got you through those tough times before, He is able to do it again. You should never find yourself not rehearsing all that He has done!

1 Chronicles 16:24 tells us to "publish his glorious deeds among the nations. Tell everyone about the amazing

things he does." You should share with others about all He has done or is doing in your life. You never know, they may be encouraged by your story! Meditating on His faithfulness will not only encourage you, but it will build your faith, and will also help you get your focus back on God instead of your current situation.

Dose for the Day

Take a moment and write down at least five things that God has done for you, and post them in places that you spend most of your time. This will serve as a much-needed reminder of God's faithfulness.

Daily Prayer

Father God,

Thank You so much for being so faithful and consistent. Everything you do is amazing. You are so good. I honor and praise you. You have done such wonderful things for me, and you are continuing to do those wonderful things in my life now. If I try to recite all of the things that you have done, I'd never stop talking! Help me to encourage myself by remembering those times when you have come through for me. I choose to remind myself of past victories won with your help. In Jesus' Name, Amen.

Scriptural References: 2 Timothy 2:13, Psalm 77:11-12, Psalm 40:5, 1 Chronicles 16:24

Who Are You?

Who are you? You are amazing. You are intelligent. You are enough. You are valuable. You are needed in the world. Most importantly, you are a child of God. 1 John 3:1 says, "What marvelous love the Father has extended to us! Just look at it—we're called children of God! That's who we really are." Your true identity should be rooted in the love of God. When you question who you are, it insults God. To question yourself is to question his ability to create something amazing. How do you see yourself? What do you think about yourself? Proverbs 23:7 says, "For as he thinks in his heart, so is he." You will never see anything new in your life until you see yourself in a new way. Jeremiah, a well-known prophet in the Bible, had doubts about his identity when God instructed him to do something. He automatically pointed out what he could not do. Jeremiah 1:5-8 says, "I knew you before I formed you in your mother's womb. Before you were born I set you apart and appointed you as my prophet to the nations." "O Sovereign Lord," I said, "I can't speak for you! I'm too young!" The Lord replied, "Don't say, 'I'm too young,' for you must go wherever I send you and say whatever I tell you. And don't be afraid of the people, for I will be with you and will protect you. I, the Lord, have spoken!" Your perception of yourself will determine every single decision you will ever make! This includes the decisions you make on your job, the type of attitude you have, the way you treat your coworkers. This is especially important in working in healthcare. There are always changes occurring and we have to adjust accordingly. If you think that you are not smart enough, skilled enough, experienced enough or strong enough to do it, then chances are you probably won't. Insecurities are rooted in fear. The solution to insecurity is a revelation of God's unconditional love. He loves and values you so much! Matthew 10:30-31 says, "And the very hairs on your head are all numbered. So don't be afraid; you are more valuable to God than a whole flock of sparrows." You are valuable!

The world identifies us by our skin color, physical traits, talents and gifts, personality, jobs, education, relationships status, our past, imperfections, etc. However, God identifies us by the Holy Spirit He placed on the inside of us when we became His. Ephesians 1:13-14 tells us, "And when you believed in Christ, he identified you as his own by giving you the Holy Spirit, whom he promised long ago. The Spirit is God's guarantee that he will give us the inheritance he promised and that he has purchased us to be his own people. He did this so we would praise and glorify him." Basically, you are perfect in His sight! I used to struggle with this reality; I depended on others, especially when it came to my career, to affirm me and to define who I was and was not. Make the decision to refuse to make this mistake. Do not use people as your point of reference. Do not rely on outside forces to define who you are. No one should have that much power over you to make you question your identity. The devil, our enemy, always questioned Jesus' identity and that is exactly how he attacks us—in the area of our identity. Why? He knows that there is nothing more dangerous or powerful than someone who knows who he or she is in Christ.

Ephesians 2:10 tells us, "For we are God's masterpiece. He has created us anew in Christ Jesus, so we can do the good things he planned for us long ago. " You were created for a purpose.

1 Peter 2:9 says, "For you are a chosen people. You are royal priests, a holy nation, God's very own possession. As a result, you can show others the goodness of God, for he called you out of the darkness into his wonderful light. " You are chosen.

Jeremiah 29:11 states, "For I know the plans I have for you," declares the Lord, "plans to prosper you and not to harm you, plans to give you hope and a future." God has a plan for your life.

Psalm 139:4-17 says, "Thank you for making me so wonderfully complex! Your workmanship is marvelous—how well I know it. You watched me as I was being formed in utter seclusion, as I was woven together in the dark of the womb. You saw me before I was born. Every day of my life was recorded in your book. Every moment was laid out before a single day had passed. How precious are your thoughts about me, O God. They cannot be numbered! " You are amazing!

Dose for the Day

Declare these affirmations over yourself today. You may want to write them down on post-it notes and place them in random places.

- I am victorious.
- I am chosen and loved by God.
- I am a child of God, whom He promises to lead.
- I am accepted.
- I am special, and I am God's good idea.
- I am the light of the world.
- I am important.
- God's thoughts about me are precious.

Daily Prayer

Father God,

Thank You for creating me with purpose. I am thankful that You love me, and call me your child. I thank You that I have no reason to struggle with my identity because You have created me and I am your idea. Your thoughts about me are precious. Help me to line up my thinking with your thoughts. I refuse to give place to the enemy by questioning my identity. I am fearless, brave, and chosen by God to be a change agent in this world. I reject and rebuke wrong thought patterns about myself. In Jesus' Name, Amen.

Scriptural References: 1 John 3:1, Jeremiah 1:5-8, Matthew 10:30-31, Ephesians 1:13-14, Ephesians 2:10, 1 Peter 2:9, Jeremiah 29:11, Psalm 139:14-17

What Did You Say?

once heard a statistic that the average number of words a person speaks per day is around 16,000. That's a lot of words. Think about it. Out of 16,000 words, how many of those words are being used to speak life and encourage others? How many of those words are used to speak defeat and failure? Are we slandering the names and character of others with our words? Believe it or not, our words have power. Proverbs 18:21 says, "Words kill, words give life; they're either poison or fruit—you choose." Proverbs 15:4 tells us, "Kind words heal and help; cutting words wound and maim." Proverbs 16:24 says, "Kind words are like honey-sweet to the soul and healthy for the body. "

Think about it. Every part of our body has a specific purpose. Our mouths are no different. Blessings and cursing should not come out of the same mouth; we shouldn't speak life and slander others with the same mouth. James 3:7-10 says, "All kinds of animals, birds, reptiles and sea creatures are being tamed and have been tamed by mankind, but no human being can tame the tongue. It is a restless evil, full of deadly poison. With the tongue we praise our Lord and Father, and with it we curse human beings, who have been made in God's likeness. Out of the same mouth come praise and cursing. My brothers and sisters, this should not be. " We should be mindful of the words that we speak. We should only speak words that are good and beneficial. According to Ephesians 4:29, "Watch the way you talk. Let nothing foul or dirty come out of your mouth. Say only what helps, each word a gift." Controlling your tongue will help you control every aspect of your life. Controlling your tongue will also preserve your life. Psalm 34:12-13 says, "Does anyone want to live a life that is long and prosperous? Then keep your tongue from speaking evil and your lips from telling lies! " Additionally, Proverbs 13:3 tells us, "Those who control their tongue will have a long life; opening your mouth can ruin everything. "

Our words also reveal what is going on in our hearts. In Matthew 15:11, Jesus says, "It's not what goes into your mouth that defiles you; you are defiled by the words that come out of your mouth." I don't necessarily believe that this scripture only references vulgar or profane words. I believe that it also applies to any word that contradicts His word.

For example, when I was applying for nurse practitioner jobs shortly after graduation, I had an opportunity to move to California for one year. I weighed my options, considered the pros and cons, and kept saying that I was, "confused, conflicted, stressed, and overwhelmed." However, God tells us that we have the mind of Christ. He gives us knowledge and understanding and has all of the wisdom that we will ever need. We have to pay attention to the things that we are saying! Be careful not to speak idle and unproductive words, such as, "It is too hard," "I am stressed out," or "This is too much for me to handle." Before speaking, ask yourself, "Is what I am about to say bringing life or death into my situation or the lives of others?

Dose for the Day

Make these declarations today. Like yesterday, you may even want to write them down on post-it notes and place them in random places!

- Death and life are in the power of the tongue, so I will be mindful of the words I speak.
- With the help of the Holy Spirit, I can control my tongue.
- I only speak words that are useful and helpful to others. Whatever I say is pleasant and kind.
- The words I speak will bring myself and others joy.
- Your words are Spirit and life, and that is what I choose to speak.
- Pleasant words are always in my mouth.
- I always have a gentle response to others.
- My words are sweet to the soul and health to my bones.
- I live a long life because I keep my tongue from speaking evil.
- I have a wholesome tongue, and it is a tree of life.

Daily Prayer

Heavenly Father,

Thank You for Your Word. Every word You speak is pure. I pray that my words are pleasing to You. I pray that every word I speak will line up with your Word. I refuse to speak any evil, but will instead speak life, hope, and peace into every situation I face. I refuse to gossip, complain, or participate in slander. I am grateful that the Holy Spirit lives on the inside of me, and helps me control what I say. My mouth will be used to declare Your mighty works and declare Your Word at all times. Help me to think before I speak. I know that death and life are in the power of the tongue and I choose life! In Jesus' Name, Amen.

Scriptural References: Proverbs 18:21, Proverbs 15:4, Proverbs 16:24, James 3:7-10, Ephesians 4:29, Psalm 34:12-13, Proverbs 13:3, Matthew 15:11

Unshakable Faith

re you hoping for something? What have you been praying for? Are you believing God for something? Maybe you are hoping for another job, a promotion, or the strength to continue where you currently are. Do you have faith that God will make it happen? Faith is a lifestyle, and it is not always easy. Hebrews 11:1 tells us, "Now faith is confidence in what we hope for and assurance about what we do not see." To have unshakable faith, you must believe that what you are praying and believing God for will come to pass—before you see it. It means that you are convinced that God will keep His Word and will come through with what He said. Hebrews 11:6 says, "It's impossible to please God apart from faith. And why? Because anyone who wants to approach God must believe both that he exists and that he cares enough to respond to those who seek him."

My favorite Biblical example of faith is Abraham and Sarah. God told them that they would have a son, even in their old age (Abraham was 100 and Sarah was 90). Initially, it was hard for them to believe it, but ultimately, they decided to put their faith in God. Hebrews 11:11 tells us, "By faith, barren Sarah was able to become pregnant, old woman as she was at the time because she believed the One who made a promise would do what he said."

According to Romans 4:18-21, "When everything was hopeless, Abraham believed anyway, deciding to live not on the basis of what he saw he couldn't do but on what God said he would do. And so, he was made father of a multitude of people. God himself said to him, "You're going to have a big family, Abraham!" Another version explains it like this: "[For Abraham, human reason for] hope being gone, hoped in faith that he should become the father of many nations, as he was promised, so [numberless] shall your descendants be. He did not weaken in faith when he considered the [utter] impotence of his own body, which was as good as dead because he was about a hundred years old, or [when he considered] the barrenness of Sarah's [deadened] womb. No unbelief or distrust made him waver (doubtingly question) concerning the promise of God, but he grew strong and was empowered by faith as he gave praise and glory to God, fully satisfied and assured that God was able and mighty to keep His word and to do what He had promised. "

Abraham's faith and belief in God grew stronger even without the manifestation of God's promise. To Abraham, God's promise was enough. If God promised it to you, it's yours. It's just that simple, no matter how difficult it may be for you to comprehend. You must remember that nothing is impossible with God. You must be confident that the things that you believe God for will happen!

1 John 5:14-15 says, "And we are confident that he hears us whenever we ask for anything that pleases him. And

since we know he hears us when we make our requests, we also know that he will give us what we ask for. " If we know the promises that God has given us and understand His character and the principles by which He works, we can pray with confidence and trust Him to grant our requests! Hebrews 10:23 says, "Let's keep a firm grip on the promises that keep us going. He always keeps his word." Decide today to refuse to entertain thoughts of doubt.

James 1:6-8 tells us, "But when you ask, you must believe and not doubt, because the one who doubts is like a wave of the sea, blown and tossed by the wind. That person should not expect to receive anything from the Lord. Such a person is double-minded and unstable in all they do. "

It doesn't matter what your situation looks like now. Be encouraged and stand firm in faith, knowing that God will come through on your behalf! "For with God nothing is ever impossible and no word from God shall be without power or impossible of fulfillment. "

Dose for the Day

Fill in the blank with whatever you believe God for!
"I am fully convinced that God will _____."

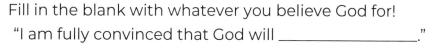

Daily Prayer

Father God,

I pray for unshakable faith. I am not faithless, but I am full of faith. I am confident in Your promises to me in Your Word. I thank You that all of Your promises are Yes and Amen. I want to thank You for everything that You have already done in my life. I am not going to wait until I see the manifestation or results; I am choosing to thank and praise You now. Help me not to doubt. Help me in those areas where unbelief takes over. I am a believer. I choose to believe Your Word. I am what Your Word says I am. I have what Your Word says I have. I can do what Your Word says I can do. I declare right now, that whatever I believe in my heart and speak with my mouth, will come to pass. I have mountain-moving faith. I am not moved by what I see or feel; I am only moved by what I believe, and I choose to believe what You have said in Your Word. In Jesus' Name, Amen.

Scriptural References: Hebrews 11:1, Hebrews 11:6, Romans 4:18-21, 1 John 5:14-15, Hebrews 10:23, James 1:6-8, Luke 1:37

DAY THIRTY- ONE
You Always Win!

I don't play sports, and I'm not the most ·competitive person in the world. However, winning makes me feel amazing! It doesn't matter if I am playing a fun game of UNO with my friends or bowling with my family, I must admit—winning is fun! Do you want to know what is not fun? Losing. A very familiar quote from a popular movie comes to mind when I think about losing: "If you're not first, you're last."

Many times in life, we feel as if we are losing. I have good news for you, my friend. As believers and children of God, you and I are on the winning team! God has already declared you victorious, so you can confidently face adversity already knowing the outcome. Romans 8:37 says that "overwhelming victory is ours through Christ, who loved us." God is for you, and He is with you. He calls you a champion before you even get in the ring. Knowing that you are victorious in Christ does something to your overall confidence and posture. 1 John 5:4 tells us, "You see, every child of God overcomes the world, for our faith is the victorious power that triumphs over the world."

As believers, we don't fight for a position of victory; we fight from a position of victory. How can we have faith in people and things that have the potential to lose but struggle to trust God who has never lost a battle? He always wins; therefore, we always win!

In 2 Kings 6, the prophet Elisha was in a tough situation and needed a quick intervention from God. He was at risk of being captured because someone lied on him. "When the servant of the man of God got up early the next morning and went outside, there were troops, horses, and chariots everywhere. "Oh, sir, what will we do now?" the young man cried to Elisha. "Don't be afraid!" Elisha told him. "For there are more on our side than on theirs!" Then Elisha prayed, "O Lord, open his eyes and let him see!" The Lord opened the young man's eyes, and when he looked up, he saw that the hillside around Elisha was filled with horses and chariots of fire. As the Aramean army advanced toward him, Elisha prayed, "O Lord, please make them blind." So, the Lord struck them with blindness as Elisha had asked. " In the end, he was supernaturally protected from his enemies' plan to attack him. When Elisha saw all of the troops on his side to protect him, he was seeing that with his spiritual eyes. The servant was scared because he was looking with his natural eyes.

We get nervous, anxious, and overwhelmed when we are faced with adversity because we are looking with our natural eyes. You must tell yourself, "No matter what it looks like, I win!" Even with eight patients by yourself, you win. Even with no help and frustrated customers, you win. Even with an unfair boss, you win. Even when you are understaffed and unsupported—you win. Overwhelming victory is yours. You win big!

Your circumstances do not determine whether you win or not. You are victorious simply because you are a child of God and He loves you unconditionally. Romans 8:35 says, "Who could ever separate us from the endless love of God's Anointed One? Absolutely no one! For nothing in the universe has the power to diminish his love toward us. Troubles, pressures, and problems are unable to come between us and heaven's love."

Dose for the Day

Make this declaration today:

"I am victorious in life. I am more than a conqueror. I am a success today and every day. God always causes me to win. Therefore, I win every battle, all of the time, every single day. Because God always causes me to win, I am a winner. I am winning now. Overwhelming victory is mine. I endure everything without weakening because the love of God in me never fails!"

Daily Prayer

Heavenly Father,

   You are amazing. Thank You for creating me to be a winner. Thank for You for making me more than a conqueror through Your love. I pray that I am successful in every area of my life. I pray that I accomplish everything that You want me to achieve because You have enabled me to do so. Fear is not a part of me, because I already know that I am going to win. You created me to do amazing things, and I am confident that I will do so. Help me not to look at my current circumstances to determine whether I will win. I am victorious because I am Your child. I thank You that I win in every single area of my life, no matter what my circumstances look like. I choose to look at my situation with my spiritual eyes instead of my natural eyes, so I can keep myself encouraged. In Jesus' Name, Amen.

Scriptural References: Romans 8:37, 1 John 5:4, 2 Kings 6:15-18, Romans 8:35

Accept Christ

If you do not have a personal relationship with God and have not proclaimed Jesus as your Lord and Savior, would you please consider it? I promise it will be the best decision you will ever make in your life. You do not have to do this alone. God loves you so much, that he sent His one and only Son to die for our sins. Romans 10:9-10 says, "If you openly declare that Jesus is Lord and believe in your heart that God raised him from the dead, you will be saved. For it is by believing in your heart that you are made right with God, and it is by openly declaring your faith that you are saved."

It is quite simple. First, you must acknowledge that you are a sinner in need of a savior. Second, you must believe in your heart that Jesus died on the cross for your sins and rose from the dead three days later. Lastly, you must confess with your mouth that Jesus Christ is your Lord and Savior.

Pray this prayer: Lord Jesus, I come to you acknowledging that I am a sinner in need of a savior. I want to be right with you. I ask that you would forgive me of all of my sins. I believe in my heart and confess with my mouth that Jesus died on the cross for my sins and was raised from the dead.

I confess that Jesus is Lord of my life. Thank you for saving me! In Jesus' Name, Amen.

Welcome to the family!

Day One: Starting Your Day

N/A

Day Two: Difficult People

The New King James Version. (1982). (1 Jn 2:6). Nashville: Thomas Nelson.

The New King James Version. (1982). (Ps 138:8). Nashville: Thomas Nelson.

Day Three: What's Love Got To Do With It?

Tyndale House Publishers. (2013). Holy Bible: New Living Translation (1 Co 13:4–7). Carol Stream, IL: Tyndale House Publishers.

Tyndale House Publishers. (2013). Holy Bible: New Living Translation (1 Jn 4:18). Carol Stream, IL: Tyndale House Publishers.

Day Four: Loved People, Love People

Peterson, E. H. (2005). The Message: the Bible in contemporary language (Jn 13:34–35). Colorado Springs, CO: NavPress.

Tyndale House Publishers. (2013). Holy Bible: New Living Translation (Mk 12:30–31). Carol Stream, IL: Tyndale House Publishers.

Tyndale House Publishers. (2013). Holy Bible: New Living Translation (1 Jn 4:7). Carol Stream, IL: Tyndale House Publishers.

Tyndale House Publishers. (2013). Holy Bible: New Living Translation (Jn 1:14). Carol Stream, IL: Tyndale House Publishers.

Tyndale House Publishers. (2013). Holy Bible: New Living Translation.

(Mt 9:12). Carol Stream, IL: Tyndale House Publishers

Tyndale House Publishers. (2013). Holy Bible: New Living Translation (Col 3:12–14). Carol Stream, IL: Tyndale House Publishers.

Simmons, B. (Trans.). (2017). The Passion Translation: New Testament (1 Co 13:4–7). BroadStreet Publishing.

Day Five: Always Be Kind

Tyndale House Publishers. (2013). Holy Bible: New Living Translation (Pr 3:3–4). Carol Stream, IL: Tyndale House Publishers.

Manser, M. H. (2009). Dictionary of Bible Themes: The Accessible and Comprehensive Tool for Topical Studies. London: Martin Manser.

Peterson, E. H. (2005). The Message: the Bible in contemporary language (Mt 9:10–13). Colorado Springs, CO: NavPress.

Tyndale House Publishers. (2013). Holy Bible: New Living Translation (Ga 5:22–23). Carol Stream, IL: Tyndale House Publishers.

Tyndale House Publishers. (2013). Holy Bible: New Living Translation (Col 3:12). Carol Stream, IL: Tyndale House Publishers.

Tyndale House Publishers. (2013). Holy Bible: New Living Translation (Ro 12:13). Carol Stream, IL: Tyndale House Publishers.

Day Six: Workplace Tea

Manser, M. H. (2009). Dictionary of Bible Themes: The Accessible and Comprehensive Tool for Topical Studies. London: Martin Manser.

Tyndale House Publishers. (2013). Holy Bible: New Living Translation (Pr 11:13). Carol Stream, IL: Tyndale House Publishers.

Tyndale House Publishers. (2013). Holy Bible: New Living Translation (Pr 16:28). Carol Stream, IL: Tyndale House Publishers.

Tyndale House Publishers. (2013). Holy Bible: New Living Translation (2 Ti 2:16–17). Carol Stream, IL: Tyndale House Publishers.

Peterson, E. H. (2005). The Message: the Bible in contemporary language (Pr 4:24). Colorado Springs, CO: NavPress.

Tyndale House Publishers. (2013). Holy Bible: New Living

Translation (1 Th 4:11–12). Carol Stream, IL: Tyndale House Publishers.

Day Seven: Up For The Challenge

The Amplified Bible. (1987). (Jn 16:33). La Habra, CA: The Lockman Foundation.

Tyndale House Publishers. (2013). Holy Bible: New Living Translation (Ps 46:10). Carol Stream, IL: Tyndale House Publishers.

Tyndale House Publishers. (2013). Holy Bible: New Living Translation (1 Th 5:16–18). Carol Stream, IL: Tyndale House Publishers.

Tyndale House Publishers. (2013). Holy Bible: New Living Translation (Is 43:2). Carol Stream, IL: Tyndale House Publishers.

Peterson, E. H. (2005). The Message: the Bible in contemporary language (1 Co 10:13). Colorado Springs, CO: NavPress.

Day Eight: Why Me?

Tyndale House Publishers. (2013). Holy Bible: New Living Translation (2 Co 4:8–9). Carol Stream, IL: Tyndale House Publishers.   Tyndale House Publishers. (2013). Holy Bible: New Living Translation (Ps 46:1). Carol Stream, IL: Tyndale House Publishers.

Tyndale House Publishers. (2013). Holy Bible: New Living Translation (Is 54:17). Carol Stream, IL: Tyndale House Publishers.

Peterson, E. H. (2005). The Message: the Bible in contemporary language (Lk 18:7–8). Colorado Springs, CO: NavPress.

Day Nine: We > Me

Tyndale House Publishers. (2013). Holy Bible: New Living Translation (Heb 10:24). Carol Stream, IL: Tyndale House Publishers.   Tyndale House Publishers. (2013). Holy Bible: New Living Translation (Nu 11:14–17). Carol Stream, IL: Tyndale House Publishers.

Peterson, E. H. (2005). The Message: the Bible in contemporary language (Ec 4:9–12). Colorado Springs, CO: NavPress.

Day Ten: Forgotten & Frustrated

Peterson, E. H. (2005). The Message: the Bible in contemporary language (Ge 16:13). Colorado Springs, CO: NavPress.

Peterson, E. H. (2005). The Message: the Bible in contemporary language (Ps 13:1–6). Colorado Springs, CO: NavPress.

Tyndale House Publishers. (2013). Holy Bible: New Living Translation (Ps 77:4–14). Carol Stream, IL: Tyndale House Publishers.

Peterson, E. H. (2005). The Message: the Bible in contemporary language (Is 49:14–15). Colorado Springs, CO: NavPress.

The New International Version. (2011). (Heb 6:10). Grand Rapids, MI: Zondervan.

The New International Version. (2011). (2 Co 10:5). Grand Rapids, MI: Zondervan.

Day Eleven: Working vs Productivity

Merriam-Webster, I. (2003). Merriam-Webster's collegiate dictionary. (Eleventh ed.). Springfield, MA: Merriam-Webster, Inc.

Merriam-Webster, I. (2003). Merriam-Webster's collegiate dictionary. (Eleventh ed.). Springfield, MA: Merriam-Webster, Inc.

Merriam-Webster, I. (2003). Merriam-Webster's collegiate dictionary. (Eleventh ed.). Springfield, MA: Merriam-Webster, Inc.

The Amplified Bible. (1987). (Pr 12:11). La Habra, CA: The Lockman Foundation.

Tyndale House Publishers. (2013). Holy Bible: New Living Translation (Eph 6:5–8). Carol Stream, IL: Tyndale House Publishers.

Tyndale House Publishers. (2013). Holy Bible: New Living Translation (Jn 15:4). Carol Stream, IL: Tyndale House Publishers.

Tyndale House Publishers. (2013). Holy Bible: New Living Translation (Ec 9:10). Carol Stream, IL: Tyndale House Publishers.

Day Twelve: Empathy Matters

Merriam-Webster, I. (2003). Merriam-Webster's collegiate dictionary. (Eleventh ed.). Springfield, MA: Merriam-Webster, Inc.

Tyndale House Publishers. (2013). Holy Bible: New Living Translation (2 Co 1:3–4). Carol Stream, IL: Tyndale House Publishers.

Tyndale House Publishers. (2013). Holy Bible: New Living Translation (Heb 4:15). Carol Stream, IL: Tyndale House Publishers.

Harris, W. H., III, Ritzema, E., Brannan, R., Mangum, D., Dunham, J., Reimer, J. A., & Wierenga, M. (Eds.). (2012). The Lexham English Bible (Mt 9:36). Bellingham, WA: Lexham Press.

Peterson, E. H. (2005). The Message: the Bible in contemporary language (Mt 9:36). Colorado Springs, CO: NavPress.

Day Thirteen: Favor

The Amplified Bible. (1987). (Ps 90:17). La Habra, CA: The Lockman Foundation.

The Holy Bible: English Standard Version. (2016). (Ge 39:21). Wheaton, IL: Crossway Bibles.

The Amplified Bible. (1987). (Ps 84:11). La Habra, CA: The Lockman Foundation.

Tyndale House Publishers. (2013). Holy Bible: New Living Translation (Ps 30:7). Carol Stream, IL: Tyndale House Publishers.

Tyndale House Publishers. (2013). Holy Bible: New Living Translation (Re 3:8). Carol Stream, IL: Tyndale House Publishers.

The Amplified Bible. (1987). (2 Pe 1:2). La Habra, CA: The Lockman Foundation.

Day Fourteen: Why Worry?

Merriam-Webster, I. (2003). Merriam-Webster's collegiate dictionary. (Eleventh ed.). Springfield, MA: Merriam-Webster, Inc.

Merriam-Webster, I. (2003). Merriam-Webster's collegiate dictionary. (Eleventh ed.). Springfield, MA: Merriam-Webster, Inc.

Manser, M. H. (2009). *Dictionary of Bible Themes: The Accessible and Comprehensive Tool for Topical Studies*. London: Martin Manser.

Tyndale House Publishers. (2013). *Holy Bible: New Living Translation* (Mt 6:31–34). Carol Stream, IL: Tyndale House Publishers.

Tyndale House Publishers. (2013). *Holy Bible: New Living Translation* (Pr 12:25). Carol Stream, IL: Tyndale House Publishers.

Peterson, E. H. (2005). *The Message: the Bible in contemporary language* (Php 4:6–7). Colorado Springs, CO: NavPress.

The Amplified Bible. (1987). (1 Pe 5:7). La Habra, CA: The Lockman Foundation.

Day Fifteen: Check Your Thoughts

The Amplified Bible. (1987). (Ro 12:2). La Habra, CA: The Lockman Foundation.

The New International Version. (2011). (2 Co 10:4–5). Grand Rapids, MI: Zondervan.

Peterson, E. H. (2005). *The Message: the Bible in contemporary language* (Php 4:8). Colorado Springs, CO: NavPress.

The Amplified Bible. (1987). (Heb 13:5). La Habra, CA: The Lockman Foundation.

Tyndale House Publishers. (2013). *Holy Bible: New Living Translation* (Je 29:11). Carol Stream, IL: Tyndale House Publishers.

Tyndale House Publishers. (2013). *Holy Bible: New Living Translation* (Ro 8:6). Carol Stream, IL: Tyndale House Publishers.

Day Sixteen: Joy

Merriam-Webster, I. (2003). *Merriam-Webster's collegiate dictionary*. (Eleventh ed.). Springfield, MA: Merriam-Webster, Inc.

Tyndale House Publishers. (2013). *Holy Bible: New Living Translation* (1 Th 5:16–18). Carol Stream, IL: Tyndale House Publishers.

Tyndale House Publishers. (2013). *Holy Bible: New Living*

Translation (Ga 5:22–23). Carol Stream, IL: Tyndale House Publishers.

The Amplified Bible. (1987). (Jn 15:10–11). La Habra, CA: The Lockman Foundation.

Tyndale House Publishers. (2013). Holy Bible: New Living Translation (Eph 1:3). Carol Stream, IL: Tyndale House Publishers.

The Holy Bible: English Standard Version. (2016). (Pr 17:22). Wheaton, IL: Crossway Bibles.

Tyndale House Publishers. (2013). Holy Bible: New Living Translation (Ne 8:10). Carol Stream, IL: Tyndale House Publishers.

Day Seventeen: What Am I Doing?

Peterson, E. H. (2005). The Message: the Bible in contemporary language (Je 29:11–14). Colorado Springs, CO: NavPress.

Tyndale House Publishers. (2013). Holy Bible: New Living Translation (Col 1:9–10). Carol Stream, IL: Tyndale House Publishers.

Tyndale House Publishers. (2013). Holy Bible: New Living Translation (Jas 1:5–8). Carol Stream, IL: Tyndale House Publishers.

Tyndale House Publishers. (2013). Holy Bible: New Living Translation (Eph 2:10). Carol Stream, IL: Tyndale House Publishers.

Tyndale House Publishers. (2013). Holy Bible: New Living Translation (Jn 4:34). Carol Stream, IL: Tyndale House Publishers.

Tyndale House Publishers. (2013). Holy Bible: New Living Translation (Eph 5:17). Carol Stream, IL: Tyndale House Publishers.

Peterson, E. H. (2005). The Message: the Bible in contemporary language (Pr 19:21). Colorado Springs, CO: NavPress.

The New King James Version. (1982). (Is 41:9–10). Nashville: Thomas Nelson.

Tyndale House Publishers. (2013). Holy Bible: New Living Translation (Ro 11:29). Carol Stream, IL: Tyndale House Publishers.

Tyndale House Publishers. (2013). Holy Bible: New Living Translation (Php 2:13). Carol Stream, IL: Tyndale House Publishers.

Tyndale House Publishers. (2013). Holy Bible: New Living Translation (Is 50:4). Carol Stream, IL: Tyndale House Publishers.

The Amplified Bible. (1987). (Pr 16:3). La Habra, CA: The Lockman Foundation.

Tyndale House Publishers. (2013). Holy Bible: New Living Translation (Ps 32:8). Carol Stream, IL: Tyndale House Publishers.

Tyndale House Publishers. (2013). Holy Bible: New Living Translation (Is 58:11). Carol Stream, IL: Tyndale House Publishers.

Day Eighteen: Be Unapologetically You

Peterson, E. H. (2005). The Message: the Bible in contemporary language (Ps 27:1). Colorado Springs, CO: NavPress.

Tyndale House Publishers. (2013). Holy Bible: New Living Translation (Php 3:3). Carol Stream, IL: Tyndale House Publishers.

Peterson, E. H. (2005). The Message: the Bible in contemporary language (Ps 139:13–18). Colorado Springs, CO: NavPress.

Tyndale House Publishers. (2013). Holy Bible: New Living Translation (Eph 2:10). Carol Stream, IL: Tyndale House Publishers.

Peterson, E. H. (2005). The Message: the Bible in contemporary language (Ro 11:29). Colorado Springs, CO: NavPress.

The Amplified Bible. (1987). (Ro 11:29). La Habra, CA: The Lockman Foundation.

Tyndale House Publishers. (2013). Holy Bible: New Living Translation (Php 4:13). Carol Stream, IL: Tyndale House Publishers.

Day Nineteen: Idle Hands

Merriam-Webster, I. (2003). Merriam-Webster's collegiate dictionary. (Eleventh ed.). Springfield, MA: Merriam-Webster, Inc.

Merriam-Webster, I. (2003). Merriam-Webster's collegiate dictionary. (Eleventh ed.). Springfield, MA: Merriam-Webster, Inc.

The Amplified Bible. (1987). (Pr 16:3). La Habra, CA: The Lockman Foundation.

Tyndale House Publishers. (2013). Holy Bible: New Living Translation (Ro 12:11–12). Carol Stream, IL: Tyndale House Publishers.

Tyndale House Publishers. (2013). Holy Bible: New Living Translation (Pr 10:4). Carol Stream, IL: Tyndale House Publishers.

Peterson, E. H. (2005). The Message: the Bible in contemporary language (Pr 12:27). Colorado Springs, CO: NavPress.

The New King James Version. (1982). (Pr 12:27). Nashville: Thomas Nelson.

Day Twenty: Shine!

Merriam-Webster, I. (2003). Merriam-Webster's collegiate dictionary. (Eleventh ed.). Springfield, MA: Merriam-Webster, Inc.

Peterson, E. H. (2005). The Message: the Bible in contemporary language (Mt 5:14–16). Colorado Springs, CO: NavPress.

Merriam-Webster, I. (2003). Merriam-Webster's collegiate dictionary. (Eleventh ed.). Springfield, MA: Merriam-Webster, Inc.

Merriam-Webster, I. (2003). Merriam-Webster's collegiate dictionary. (Eleventh ed.). Springfield, MA: Merriam-Webster, Inc.

Tyndale House Publishers. (2013). Holy Bible: New Living Translation (1 Jn 1:5). Carol Stream, IL: Tyndale House Publishers.

Tyndale House Publishers. (2013). Holy Bible: New Living Translation (Jn 8:12). Carol Stream, IL: Tyndale House Publishers.

Tyndale House Publishers. (2013). Holy Bible: New Living Translation (Col 3:17). Carol Stream, IL: Tyndale House Publishers.

Tyndale House Publishers. (2013). Holy Bible: New Living Translation (Eph 5:8–9). Carol Stream, IL: Tyndale House Publishers.

Tyndale House Publishers. (2013). Holy Bible: New Living Translation (Php 2:15). Carol Stream, IL: Tyndale House Publishers.

Day Twenty-One: Make Time

The Amplified Bible. (1987). (Mt 11:28–30). La Habra, CA: The Lockman Foundation.

Peterson, E. H. (2005). *The Message: the Bible in contemporary language* (Mt 11:28–30). Colorado Springs, CO: NavPress.

The New International Version. (2011). (2 Co 10:5). Grand Rapids, MI: Zondervan.

The New International Version. (2011). (Ge 2:2). Grand Rapids, MI: Zondervan.

Tyndale House Publishers. (2013). *Holy Bible: New Living Translation* (Heb 4:9–11). Carol Stream, IL: Tyndale House Publishers.

Day Twenty-Two: Graced for This

Peterson, E. H. (2005). *The Message: the Bible in contemporary language* (1 Co 15:10). Colorado Springs, CO: NavPress.

Tyndale House Publishers. (2013). *Holy Bible: New Living Translation* (Eph 1:3). Carol Stream, IL: Tyndale House Publishers.

Tyndale House Publishers. (2013). *Holy Bible: New Living Translation* (Ro 12:6). Carol Stream, IL: Tyndale House Publishers.

Tyndale House Publishers. (2013). *Holy Bible: New Living Translation* (Ro 11:6). Carol Stream, IL: Tyndale House Publishers.

Peterson, E. H. (2005). *The Message: the Bible in contemporary language* (2 Co 12:9–10). Colorado Springs, CO: NavPress.

Tyndale House Publishers. (2013). *Holy Bible: New Living Translation* (Heb 4:15–16). Carol Stream, IL: Tyndale House Publishers.

Day Twenty-Three: Ultimate Boss

Peterson, E. H. (2005). *The Message: the Bible in contemporary language* (Col 3:22–24). Colorado Springs, CO: NavPress.

Tyndale House Publishers. (2013). *Holy Bible: New Living Translation* (Ro 12:11). Carol Stream, IL: Tyndale House Publishers.

Tyndale House Publishers. (2013). *Holy Bible: New Living Translation* (1 Ti 2:2). Carol Stream, IL: Tyndale House Publishers.

Tyndale House Publishers. (2013). *Holy Bible: New Living Translation* (Pr 21:1). Carol Stream, IL: Tyndale House Publishers.

Tyndale House Publishers. (2013). Holy Bible: New Living Translation (Ps 37:23). Carol Stream, IL: Tyndale House Publishers.

The Amplified Bible. (1987). (Heb 13:5–6). La Habra, CA: The Lockman Foundation.

The Amplified Bible. (1987). (Php 2:13). La Habra, CA: The Lockman Foundation.

The Amplified Bible. (1987). (Is 40:28–29). La Habra, CA: The Lockman Foundation.

Tyndale House Publishers. (2013). Holy Bible: New Living Translation (Nu 23:19). Carol Stream, IL: Tyndale House Publishers.

Tyndale House Publishers. (2013). Holy Bible: New Living Translation (Ps 89:34). Carol Stream, IL: Tyndale House Publishers.

Day Twenty-Four: UGH!

Merriam-Webster, I. (2003). Merriam-Webster's collegiate dictionary. (Eleventh ed.). Springfield, MA: Merriam-Webster, Inc.

Merriam-Webster, I. (2003). Merriam-Webster's collegiate dictionary. (Eleventh ed.). Springfield, MA: Merriam-Webster, Inc.

Tyndale House Publishers. (2013). Holy Bible: New Living Translation (Is 26:3). Carol Stream, IL: Tyndale House Publishers.

Tyndale House Publishers. (2013). Holy Bible: New Living Translation (Ps 29:11). Carol Stream, IL: Tyndale House Publishers.

The Amplified Bible. (1987). (Ps 4:8). La Habra, CA: The Lockman Foundation.

Tyndale House Publishers. (2013). Holy Bible: New Living Translation (Ps 112:7). Carol Stream, IL: Tyndale House Publishers.

Tyndale House Publishers. (2013). Holy Bible: New Living Translation (Php 4:6–7). Carol Stream, IL: Tyndale House Publishers.

Day Twenty-Five: Scared Straight

The Amplified Bible. (1987). (2 Ti 1:7). La Habra, CA: The Lockman Foundation.

The Amplified Bible. (1987). (1 Jn 4:18). La Habra, CA: The Lockman Foundation.

Tyndale House Publishers. (2013). Holy Bible: New Living Translation (Jn 6:19–21). Carol Stream, IL: Tyndale House Publishers.

Peterson, E. H. (2005). The Message: the Bible in contemporary language (Is 41:10). Colorado Springs, CO: NavPress.

The Amplified Bible. (1987). (Is 41:13). La Habra, CA: The Lockman Foundation.

Tyndale House Publishers. (2013). Holy Bible: New Living Translation (Dt 31:6). Carol Stream, IL: Tyndale House Publishers.

Tyndale House Publishers. (2013). Holy Bible: New Living Translation (Ps 34:4). Carol Stream, IL: Tyndale House Publishers.

Peterson, E. H. (2005). The Message: the Bible in contemporary language (Ps 34:4). Colorado Springs, CO: NavPress.

Tyndale House Publishers. (2013). Holy Bible: New Living Translation (Ps 56:3–4). Carol Stream, IL: Tyndale House Publishers.

Peterson, E. H. (2005). The Message: the Bible in contemporary language (Je 32:27). Colorado Springs, CO: NavPress.

Day Twenty-Six: The Best Conversation

Tyndale House Publishers. (2013). Holy Bible: New Living Translation (1 Th 5:16–17). Carol Stream, IL: Tyndale House Publishers.

Peterson, E. H. (2005). The Message: the Bible in contemporary language (Php 4:6–7). Colorado Springs, CO: NavPress.

Tyndale House Publishers. (2013). Holy Bible: New Living Translation (Col 4:2). Carol Stream, IL: Tyndale House Publishers.

Tyndale House Publishers. (2013). Holy Bible: New Living Translation (Eph 6:18). Carol Stream, IL: Tyndale House Publishers.

Tyndale House Publishers. (2013). Holy Bible: New Living Translation (Jas 5:16). Carol Stream, IL: Tyndale House Publishers.

The New International Version. (2011). (1 Jn 5:14–15). Grand Rapids, MI: Zondervan.

Peterson, E. H. (2005). The Message: the Bible in contemporary language (Ps 145:18). Colorado Springs, CO: NavPress.

Peterson, E. H. (2005). The Message: the Bible in contemporary language (Eph 6:18). Colorado Springs, CO: NavPress.

Day Twenty-Seven: Remember the Time

Tyndale House Publishers. (2013). Holy Bible: New Living Translation (2 Ti 2:13). Carol Stream, IL: Tyndale House Publishers.

Tyndale House Publishers. (2013). Holy Bible: New Living Translation (Ps 77:11–12). Carol Stream, IL: Tyndale House Publishers.

Tyndale House Publishers. (2013). Holy Bible: New Living Translation (Ps 40:5). Carol Stream, IL: Tyndale House Publishers.

Tyndale House Publishers. (2013). Holy Bible: New Living Translation (1 Ch 16:24). Carol Stream, IL: Tyndale House Publishers.

Day Twenty-Eight: Who Are You?

Peterson, E. H. (2005). The Message: the Bible in contemporary language (1 Jn 3:1). Colorado Springs, CO: NavPress.

The New King James Version. (1982). (Pr 23:7). Nashville: Thomas Nelson.

Tyndale House Publishers. (2013). Holy Bible: New Living Translation (Je 1:5–8). Carol Stream, IL: Tyndale House Publishers.

Tyndale House Publishers. (2013). Holy Bible: New Living Translation (Mt 10:30–31). Carol Stream, IL: Tyndale House Publishers.

Tyndale House Publishers. (2013). Holy Bible: New Living Translation (Eph 1:13–14). Carol Stream, IL: Tyndale House Publishers.

Tyndale House Publishers. (2013). Holy Bible: New Living Translation (Eph 2:10). Carol Stream, IL: Tyndale House Publishers.

Tyndale House Publishers. (2013). Holy Bible: New Living Translation (1 Pe 2:9). Carol Stream, IL: Tyndale House Publishers.

The New International Version. (2011). (Je 29:11). Grand Rapids, MI: Zondervan.

Tyndale House Publishers. (2013). Holy Bible: New Living Translation (Ps 139:14–17). Carol Stream, IL: Tyndale House Publishers.

Day Twenty-Nine: What Did You Say?

Peterson, E. H. (2005). The Message: the Bible in contemporary language (Pr 18:21). Colorado Springs, CO: NavPress.

Peterson, E. H. (2005). The Message: the Bible in contemporary language (Pr 15:4). Colorado Springs, CO: NavPress.

Tyndale House Publishers. (2013). Holy Bible: New Living Translation (Pr 16:24). Carol Stream, IL: Tyndale House Publishers.

The New International Version. (2011). (Jas 3:7–10). Grand Rapids, MI: Zondervan.

Peterson, E. H. (2005). The Message: the Bible in contemporary language (Eph 4:29). Colorado Springs, CO: NavPress.

Tyndale House Publishers. (2013). Holy Bible: New Living Translation (Ps 34:12–13). Carol Stream, IL: Tyndale House Publishers.

Tyndale House Publishers. (2013). Holy Bible: New Living Translation (Pr 13:3). Carol Stream, IL: Tyndale House Publishers.

Tyndale House Publishers. (2013). Holy Bible: New Living Translation (Mt 15:11). Carol Stream, IL: Tyndale House Publishers.

Day Thirty: Unshakable Faith

The New International Version. (2011). (Heb 11:1). Grand Rapids, MI: Zondervan.

Peterson, E. H. (2005). The Message: the Bible in contemporary language (Heb 11:6). Colorado Springs, CO: NavPress.

Peterson, E. H. (2005). The Message: the Bible in contemporary language (Heb 11:11). Colorado Springs, CO: NavPress.

Peterson, E. H. (2005). The Message: the Bible in contemporary language (Ro 4:18). Colorado Springs, CO: NavPress.

The Amplified Bible. (1987). (Ro 4:18–21). La Habra, CA: The Lockman Foundation.

Tyndale House Publishers. (2013). Holy Bible: New Living Translation (1 Jn 5:14–15). Carol Stream, IL: Tyndale House Publishers.

Peterson, E. H. (2005). The Message: the Bible in contemporary language (Heb 10:23). Colorado Springs, CO: NavPress.

The New International Version. (2011). (Jas 1:6–8). Grand Rapids, MI: Zondervan.

The Amplified Bible. (1987). (Lk 1:37). La Habra, CA: The Lockman Foundation.

Day Thirty-One: You Always Win!

Tyndale House Publishers. (2013). Holy Bible: New Living Translation (Ro 8:37). Carol Stream, IL: Tyndale House Publishers.

Simmons, B. (Trans.). (2017). The Passion Translation: New Testament (1 Jn 5:4). BroadStreet Publishing.

Tyndale House Publishers. (2013). Holy Bible: New Living Translation (2 Ki 6:15–18). Carol Stream, IL: Tyndale House Publishers.

Simmons, B. (Trans.). (2017). The Passion Translation: New Testament (Ro 8:35). BroadStreet Publishing.

About the Author

A native of Huntsville, Alabama, Danielle Barnes dedicates her life and career to serving others. A strong desire to serve and her intense love for people developed her passion for educating people about health awareness.

She graduated from the University of Alabama at Birmingham in 2008 with a Bachelor of Science in Nursing. After working as a registered nurse in the Birmingham metro area, Danielle began working as a travel nurse. Her travel nursing endeavor took her across state lines, but she eventually made her way back to Alabama. Shortly after returning home, Danielle began pursuing her master's degree in nursing and became a Board Certified Family Nurse Practitioner in 2017.

Throughout her career, Danielle has received many awards for her exemplary work including a nomination for the DAISY Award for Extraordinary Nurses. Danielle is also a member of Sigma Theta Tau, the Honor Society of Nursing. She currently lives in Huntsville, where she is an active member in her community and church, and practices as a family nurse practitioner.

Acknowledgments

To my amazing parents, Danny and Vivian: Thank you both for teaching me at an early age the importance of including God in my everyday life. Thank you for speaking life into my dreams and aspirations, and for your priceless wisdom. I appreciate your love, support, and endless prayers. I am extremely blessed to have you both in my life. I love you!

To my one and only brother, Daniel: Thank you for your constant support and encouragement, as well as keeping me up to date on pop culture. Seeing you go hard after all God has for you inspires me more than you know. I'm so proud of you. Big sis loves you so much!

To my family – my Grandma, as well as all of my aunts, uncles, and cousins – I am so blessed to have such a loving and supportive family. I love each of you dearly!

To my beautiful best friends – Tracey, Brittany, and Ivory – I love each of you so much! I am so grateful for your friendship. You are more than my friends, you are my sisters. Thank you for your love, support, time, accountability, and the endless laughs. My life is better because you all are in it.

Finally, to all of my fellow healthcare professionals who

read my book, THANK YOU! It is my prayer that this devotional helps you and encourages you to keep going. God bless you!

Stay Connected

Thank you for reading *Daily Doses*. Danielle looks forward to connecting with you and keeping you updated on her next releases. Below are a few ways you can connect with the author.

FACEBOOK Danielle Barnes
INSTAGRAM ali.danielle
WEBSITE www.thedaniellebarnes.com

Made in the USA
Columbia, SC
20 April 2020